D0938863

Modern Critical Interpretations

George Eliot's
The Mill on the Floss

Modern Critical Interpretations

These and other titles in preparation

Modern Critical Interpretations

George Eliot's

The Mill on the Floss

Edited and with an introduction by
Harold Bloom
Sterling Professor of the Humanities
Yale University

Chelsea House Publishers ◊ *1988*
NEW YORK ◊ NEW HAVEN ◊ PHILADELPHIA

© 1988 by Chelsea House Publishers, a division
of Chelsea House Educational Communications, Inc.,
   95 Madison Avenue, New York, NY 10016
   345 Whitney Avenue, New Haven, CT 06511
   5068B West Chester Pike, Edgemont, PA 19028

Introduction © 1988 by Harold Bloom

Printed and bound in the United States of America

10 9 8 7 6 5 4 3 2 1

∞ The paper used in this publication meets the minimum
requirements of the American National Standard for Permanence
of Paper for Printed Library Materials, Z39.48–1984.

Library of Congress Cataloging-in-Publication Data
George Eliot's The mill on the floss / edited and with an
 introduction by Harold Bloom.
     p.   cm. — (Modern critical interpretations)
   Bibliography: p.
   Includes index.
   ISBN 0–87754–740–8 (alk. paper) : $19.95
   1. Eliot, George, 1819–1880.   Mill on the Floss.   I. Bloom,
Harold.   II. Series.
 PR4664.G45   1988
 823'.8—dc19   87–18364
                                                              CIP

Contents

Editor's Note

This book brings together a representative selection of the best modern critical interpretations of George Eliot's novel *The Mill on the Floss*. The critical essays are reprinted here in the chronological order of their original publication. I am grateful to Kevin Pask for his assistance in editing this volume.

My introduction centers upon Eliot's moral stance of renunciation, and speculates upon its relation to Maggie's shocking death. George Levine begins the chronological sequence of criticism with his meditations upon what he terms Eliot's "complex mode of self-deceit" in the novel.

In U. C. Knoepflmacher's reading, *The Mill on the Floss* is judged to be less than a tragedy primarily because Maggie's drowning makes her a figure of pathos, a victim of capricious and accidental forces. Nina Auerbach, questing for the demonic, uncovers it in Maggie's uncanny powers of sight and vision, emblematic of a hunger for love fused with the death drive.

Subtly arguing that feminist criticism illuminates by its utopianism, Mary Jacobus nevertheless admits the absence in *The Mill on the Floss* of "a specifically feminine linguistic practice." Dianne F. Sadoff finds in Mr. Tulliver the figure of the failed father, and in Maggie the image of the daughter who subsequently undergoes a cycle of desire and punishment.

Wordsworth's strong influence upon George Eliot is analyzed as Eliot's revisionary agon of ambivalence by Margaret Homans, who darkly suggests "that the inevitability of women's variance from the Wordsworthian model brings, not only power, but also pain." In this volume's final essay, Gillian Beer raises the even darker problem: is the representation of female heroism in literature to be confined to martyrdom? Her tentative answer, at least with regard to George Eliot, is that heroines after Maggie may renounce, but essentially survive, and find other significant forms of heroic activity.

Introduction

> *Even taken in its derivative meaning of outline, what is form but the limit of*
> *that difference by which we discriminate one object from another?—a limit*
> *determined partly by the intrinsic relations or composition of the object, &*
> *partly by the extrinsic action of other bodies upon it. This is true whether the*
> *object is a rock or a man . . .*
> GEORGE ELIOT, "Notes on Forms in Art"

It was Freud, in our time, who taught us again what the pre-Socratics taught: *ethos* is the *daimon*, character is fate. A generation before Freud, George Eliot taught the same unhappy truth to her contemporaries. If character is fate, then in a harsh sense there can be no accidents. Character presumably is less volatile than personality, and we tend to disdain anyone who would say: personality is fate. Personalities suffer accidents; characters endure fate. If we seek major personalities among the great novelists, we find many competitors: Balzac, Tolstoy, Dickens, Henry James, even the enigmatic Conrad. By general agreement, the grand instance of a moral character would be George Eliot. She has a nearly unique spiritual authority, best characterized by the English critic Walter Allen about twenty years ago:

> George Eliot is the first novelist in the world in some things,
> and they are the things that come within the scope of her
> moral interpretation of life. Circumscribed though it was, it
> was certainly not narrow; nor did she ever forget the difficulty
> attendant upon the moral life and the complexity that goes to
> its making.

Her peculiar gift, almost unique despite her place in a tradition of displaced Protestantism that includes Samuel Richardson's *Clarissa* and Wordsworth's poetry, is to dramatize her interpretations in such a way as to abolish the demarcations between aesthetic pleasure and moral renunciation. Richardson's heroine, Clarissa Harlowe, and Wordsworth in

1

his best poems share in a compensatory formula: experiential loss can be transformed into imaginative gain. Eliot's imagination, despite its Words-worthian antecedents, and despite the ways in which Clarissa Harlowe is the authentic precursor of Dorothea Brooke in *Middlemarch,* is too severe to accept the formula of compensation. The beauty of renunciation in Eliot's fiction does not result from a transformation of loss, but rather from a strength that is in no way dependent upon exchange or gain. Eliot presents us with the puzzle of what might be called the Moral Sublime. To her contemporaries, this was no puzzle. F. W. H. Myers, remembered now as a "psychic researcher" (a marvelous metaphor that we oddly use as a title for those who quest after spooks) and as the father of L. H. Myers, author of the novel *The Near and the Far,* wrote a famous descrip-tion of Eliot's 1873 visit to Cambridge:

> I remember how at Cambridge I walked with her once in the Fellows' Garden of Trinity, on an evening of rainy May; and she, stirred somewhat beyond her wont, and taking as her text the three words which had been used so often as the inspiring trumpet-call of men—the words God, Immortality, Duty—pronounced with terrible earnestness how inconceivable was the first, how unbelievable was the second, and yet how per-emptory and absolute the third. Never, perhaps, have sterner accents confirmed the sovereignty of impersonal and unre-compensing Law. I listened, and night fell; her grave, majestic countenance turned towards me like a sybil's in the gloom; it was as though she withdrew from my grasp, one by one, the two scrolls of promise and left me the third scroll only, awful with inevitable fates. And when we stood at length and parted, amid that columnar circuit of forest trees, beneath the last twilight of starless skies, I seemed to be gazing, like Titus at Jerusalem, on vacant seats and empty halls—on a sanctuary with no Presence to hallow it, and heaven left empty of God.

However this may sound now, Myers intended no ironies. As the sybil of "unrecompensing Law," Eliot joined the austere company of nineteenth-century prose prophets: Carlyle, Ruskin, Newman, and Ar-nold in England; Emerson in America; Schopenhauer, Nietzsche, Kier-kegaard, and finally Freud on the Continent. But this ninefold, though storytellers of a sort, wrote no novels. Eliot's deepest affinities were scarcely with Dickens, Thackeray, and Trollope, and yet her formal achievement requires us to read her as we read them. This causes difficulties, since Eliot was not a great stylist, and was far more immersed in philosophical than in narrative tradition. Yet her frequent clumsiness in authorial asides and her hesitations in storytelling matter not at all. We do not even regret her absolute lack of any sense of the comic, which never dares take revenge upon her anyway. Wordsworth at his strongest, as in "Resolution and Independence," still can be unintentionally funny (which inspired the splendid parodies of the poem's leech-gatherer and its solipsistic bard in Lewis Carroll's "White Knight's Ballad," and Edward Lear's "Incidents in the Life of my uncle Arly"). But I have seen no effective parodies of George Eliot, and doubt their possibility. It is usually unwise to be witty concerning our desperate need, not only to decide upon right action, but also to will such action, against pleasure and against what we take to be self-interest. Like Freud, Eliot ultimately is an inescapable moralist, precisely delineating our discomfort with culture, and remorselessly weighing the economics of the psyche's civil wars.

II

George Eliot is not one of the great letter writers. Her letters matter because they are hers, and in some sense do tell part of her own story, but they do not yield to a continuous reading. On a scale of nineteenth-century letter-writing by important literary figures, in which Keats would rank first, and Walter Pater last (the Paterian prose style is never present in his letters), Eliot would find a place about dead center. She is always herself in her letters, too much herself perhaps, but that self is rugged, honest, and formidably inspiring. Our contemporary feminist critics seem to me a touch uncomfortable with Eliot. Here she is on extending the franchise to women, in a letter to John Morley (May 14, 1867):

> Thanks for your kind practical remembrance. Your attitude in relation to Female Enfranchisement seems to be very nearly mine. If I were called on to act in the matter, I would certainly not oppose any plan which held out a reasonable promise of tending to establish as far as possible an equivalence of advantages for the two sexes, as to education and the possibilities of free development. I fear you may have misunderstood something I said the other evening about nature. I never meant to urge the "intention of Nature" argument, which is to me a

pitiable fallacy. I mean that as a fact of mere zoological evolution, woman seems to me to have the worst share in existence. But for that very reason I would the more contend that in the moral evolution we have "an art which does mend nature"—an art which "itself is nature." It is the function of love in the largest sense, to mitigate the harshness of all fatalities. And in the thorough recognition of that worse share, I think there is a basis for a sublimer resignation in woman and a more regenerating tenderness in man.

However, I repeat that I do not trust very confidently to my own impressions on this subject. The peculiarities of my own lot may have caused me to have idiosyncrasies rather than an average judgment. The one conviction on the matter which I hold with some tenacity is, that through all transitions the goal towards which we are proceeding is a more clearly discerned distinctness of function (allowing always for exceptional cases of individual organization) with as near an approach to equivalence of good for woman and for man as can be secured by the effort of growing moral force to lighten the pressure of hard non-moral outward conditions. It is rather superfluous, perhaps injudicious, to plunge into such deeps as these in a hasty note, but it is difficult to resist the desire to botch imperfect talk with a little imperfect writing.

This is a strong insistence upon form in life as in art, upon the limit of that difference by which we discriminate one object from another. I have heard feminist critics decry it as defeatism, though Eliot speaks of "mere zoological evolution" as bringing about every woman's "worse share in existence." "A sublimer resignation in woman" is not exactly a popular goal these days, but Eliot never speaks of the sublime without profundity and an awareness of human loss. When she praises Ruskin as a teacher "with the inspiration of a Hebrew prophet," she also judges him to be "strongly akin to the sublimest part of Wordsworth," a judgment clearly based upon the Wordsworthian source of Ruskin's tropes for the sense of loss that dominates the sublime experience. The harshness of being a woman, however mitigated by societal reform, will remain, Eliot reminds us, since we cannot mend nature and its unfairness. Her allusion to the Shakespearean "art which does mend nature," and which "itself is nature" (*Winter's Tale*, 4.4.88–96) subtly emends Shakespeare in the deliberately wistful hope for a moral evolution of love between the sexes. What dominates this letter to Morley is a harsh plangency, yet it is anything but defeatism. Perhaps Eliot should have spoken of a "resigned sublimity" rather than a "sublime resignation," but her art, and life, give the lie to any contemporary feminist demeaning of the author of *Middlemarch,* who shares with Jane Austen and Emily Dickinson the eminence of being the strongest women writers in the English language.

III

The *Mill on the Floss* (1860) is George Eliot's strongest achievement before *Middlemarch* (1871–72) and remains a vital novel by any standards. Rereading it confirms my earlier annoyance at its inadequate conclusion, the drowning of the heroine Maggie Tulliver, and her beloved brother Tom, by the Floss river in full flood. But this seems the only substantial blemish in one of the major autobiographical novels in the language, comparable to Dickens's *David Copperfield* and prophetic of Lawrence's *Sons and Lovers.* The splendor of *The Mill on the Floss* is almost entirely in Eliot's portrayal of her own earlier phases in the intensely sympathetic Maggie, whose death most readers fiercely resent. There is no tragic necessity in Maggie's drowning, and I do not believe that literary criticism is capable of explaining why Eliot made so serious a blunder, though recently feminist critics have ventured upon correcting some of Eliot's perspectives. Moral criticism of George Eliot, in my judgment, does not work very well, since the critic, of whatever gender or ideological persuasion, presumes to enter upon a contest with the most formidable and imaginative moralist in the history of the British novel.

I myself can only speculate upon why Eliot decided to destroy her earlier self by drowning the humane and luminous Maggie. Certainly it was not because the novelist could not imagine a form of life for her surrogate self. Maggie moves us most because her yearning demand is for more life, for a sublime relationship to herself, to other selves and to the world. Dr. F. R. Leavis, who made of an ill-defined "maturity" a critical shibboleth, decided that Maggie was immature and lacked self-knowledge, and so must have reflected a phase in Eliot's development when she was not yet worthy of Leavisite endorsement. Rereading *The Mill on the Floss* is likelier to show the reader that Maggie has a healthy sexual nature and does the best she can for herself in a harsh society, while ultimately restrained by the considerable moral perplexities of her own passionately divided psyche. The center of Maggie's dilemma is her erotic attachment to Stephen Guest, a whipping-boy for critics from

Eliot's contemporaries on to ours. Readers of *The Mill on the Floss* need to ask why George Eliot has Maggie renounce Stephen, before they can ask why the author concludes by Maggie's gratuitous death.

"Renunciation," as Emily Dickinson wrote with wit grand and grim, "is a piercing virtue," and perhaps it killed Maggie Tulliver, which is a curious paradox at best, since George Eliot consciously cannot have intended some causal connection between her heroine's abandonment of sexual happiness and subsequent drowning in her brother's embrace. Yet there is an authentic link between the almost unmotivated renunciation and the arbitrarily imposed conclusion. We sense that if Maggie had married Stephen, the Floss would not have flooded. That is an outrageous sentence, I suppose, but not nearly so outrageous as the renunciation, which is a self-violation rather than a self-sacrifice on Maggie's part. And the renunciation, though senseless, is far short of the sentimental outrageousness of the conclusion, with its veiled metaphor of incestuous passion:

> Nothing else was said; a new danger was being carried towards them by the river. Some wooden machinery had just given way on one of the wharves, and huge fragments were being floated along. The sun was rising now, and the wide area of watery desolation was spread out in dreadful clearness around them—in dreadful clearness floated onwards the hurrying, threatening masses. A large company in a boat that was working its way along under the Tofton houses, observed their danger, and shouted, "Get out of the current!"
>
> But that could not be done at once, and Tom, looking before him, saw Death rushing on them. Huge fragments, clinging together in fatal fellowship, made one wide mass across the stream.
>
> "It is coming, Maggie!" Tom said, in a deep hoarse voice, loosing the oars, and clasping her.
>
> The next instant the boat was no longer seen upon the water—and the huge mass was hurrying on in hideous triumph.
>
> But soon the keel of the boat reappeared, a black speck on the golden water.
>
> The boat reappeared—but brother and sister had gone down in an embrace never to be parted—living through again in one supreme moment, the days when they had clasped their little hands in love, and roamed the daisied fields together.

"Clinging together in fatal fellowship" is the darkly revelatory emphasis of this ending, which compels the reader to surmise that the repressed motive for the renunciation of Stephen was the attachment between sister and brother.

"One supreme moment," since sexual union is barred, has to be mutual immolation. This may seem more like the Shelley of *The Revolt of Islam* than the Wordsworth of *The Excursion,* and certainly would have been rejected as an interpretation by George Eliot herself. But it may help explain so wayward and inadequate a culmination to a novel otherwise worthy of the intense and varied existence, tragically brief, of Maggie Tulliver.

Intelligence as Deception:
The Mill on the Floss

George Levine

With only small exceptions, *The Mill on the Floss* can be seen as adequately representative of even the most mature of George Eliot's art—morally energetic yet unsentimentally perceptive about the meaning of experience. Like all of her works, it is thoroughly coherent and gains its coherence from a unified vision. But the vision, here as elsewhere, is, I would argue, incomplete. There were elements in experience, that is, which she was never fully able to assimilate and which, as was true of most of the major Victorian writers, she was genuinely unable to see. She pushed the boundaries of Victorian experience as far as any of her contemporaries and moved to the brink from which one can observe the modern sensibility, but inevitably she pulled back.

The point at which she stopped is the point at which *The Mill on the Floss*—which remains one of the very great novels of the period—goes wrong. The difficulty, I would suggest, is not merely George Eliot's excessive moral energy nor even, exclusively, her too close identification, criticised by F. R. Leavis, with her heroine. Rather, it seems to me to result from a complex mode of self-deceit—from a combination of high intelligence with powerful moral revulsion from what that intelligence tended to reveal.

I

It is important, at the outset, to remember that George Eliot's intelligence was at home with several highly elaborated intellectual systems

From *PMLA* 80, no. 4 (September 1965). © 1965 by the Modern Language Association of America.

which, she believed, could largely—if not entirely—account for the experience being narrated. Of course, her works cannot be reduced simply to any one set of rationally coherent ideas; but it is certainly true that her empirical and rationalist biases (modified though they were by her total commitment to "truth of feeling") demanded an explanation of experience consistent with reason, and that the explanation she accepted influenced certain crucial elements in her novels. Determinism is the central and dominant explanation of the facts of the experience; the moral direction of those facts is controlled largely by many ideas which might be traced to Comte and Feuerbach. All of these ideas are woven inextricably into the very texture of *The Mill on the Floss,* but I shall argue that there came a recognizable point at which, especially in her use of Feuerbach, George Eliot employs them in such a way as to help her escape the implications of her own most deeply felt insights.

To begin with, then, it is necessary to clarify what the informing ideas of *The Mill on the Floss* meant to George Eliot. For her, determinism, as I have explained elsewhere, entailed a total commitment to the notion that every action has its causes, and only by a meticulous examination of those causes can any action be seen as comprehensible. She also argued, however, that determinism does not entail belief in inefficacy of the will. Since, that is, a man's character is always an element in his choice, he must be seen as responsible. Finally, whatever the intellectual formulation might be, to excuse a man on the basis of an abstract theory of determinism is altogether irrelevant to his evil; as Adam Bede remarks, "I see plain enough we shall never do it without a resolution, and that's enough for me."

All the major themes of *The Mill on the Floss,* as well as its structure, are related to determinism. It is a commonplace that the novel develops as Tom and Maggie grow: it sets them within the framework of a family and society which extensively determine what they become, shows the inevitable development of their characters according to the pressures of heredity and irrevocable events, and traces their destinies chronologically from love, to division, to unity in death. The simple narrative progression is incremental and stresses the ineluctable dependence of every act and thought on acts and thoughts which preceded them.

Both in its personal drama and in its vividly imagined description of a period of social transition the novel seems illustrative also of many of Comte's and Feuerbach's notions of social and moral growth. In a letter to John Blackwood comparing *Adam Bede* to *The Mill on the Floss,* which was then in progress, George Eliot noted that the characters in the latter "are on a lower level generally." Quite deliberately, she was creating a society which has not as yet moved beyond the egoism of man's animal beginnings to the sympathy and benevolence which Feuerbach and Comte believed would grow out of egoism. Among other things, the frequency with which all the characters are compared to insects and animals makes plain that George Eliot does not see them as ready for any but the slightest advance toward the full intellectual and moral development from egoism to intelligent sympathy towards which she aspired.

Aside from working out George Eliot's characteristic theme of "the adjustment of our individual needs to the dire necessities of our lot," Maggie's story is also a dramatization of Feuerbach's religion of suffering—the "suffering, whether of martyr or victim, which belongs to every historical advance of mankind" (bk. 4, chap. 1). Through suffering the "obscure vitality" of the "emmet-like Dodsons and Tullivers" will be transcended, will be "swept into the same oblivion with the generations of ants and beavers," and man will move slowly towards his full humanity. The immersion in water, which in the final chapter is the form which the suffering takes, is, in Feuerbach's view, an annihilation of consciousness: it is the first step towards regeneration, but the regeneration itself must be active, not passive, the assertion of "the power of mind, of consciousness, of man." Maggie's world lacks the moral guidance Comte insisted was necessary for that regeneration or for the achievement of a satisfactory society: it had "no standard but hereditary custom" (bk. 4, chap. 1).

Ideas such as these form the intellectual framework of *The Mill on the Floss*. The ideas and the experience, however, are two aspects of the same thing. Here at least one feels no tension between the two halves of the almost schizophrenic (intellectual vs. emotional) George Eliot that critics have taken to creating. For all but a brief section of the book the experience itself seems a necessary and convincing source of the ideas; although the world the novel describes is entirely deterministic and largely positivistic, the "system" does not distort the experience. But since the details of the novel are so widely known, I shall concentrate on the relation between the ideas and the experience—rather than on the experience itself—in order to suggest how George Eliot's extraordinarily tough-minded and complicated analysis of personal and social experience could have concluded in a "comfortingly conventional" way, "its tone barely distinguishable from hundreds of pious and exemplary tales where salvation comes through sacrifice and love triumphs over death."

II

George Eliot's "love of the childhood scenes" is not likely to have carried her to such lengthy description as we have in the early books had she not felt those scenes were important, both intrinsically and for the development of the novel as a whole. They are in fact a demonstration of the idea which she found confirmed in Comte, of whom she said that "no one has more clearly seen the truth, that the past rules the present, lives in it, and that we are but the growth and outcome of the past." The focus on family in the first book relates directly to the Comtean notion (shared by Feuerbach) that the family is the primary means by which man can transcend his egoism and animality. These early scenes establish that the characters are, in Feuerbach's terms, in a "natural" state, beneath the level of full humanity. It is no accident, for example, that the novel's first speech by an important character—Mr. Tulliver—should begin, "What I want," nor that George Eliot should pointedly repeat the clause (bk. 1, chap. 2). "The oppressive narrowness" of the Dodsons and Tullivers creates a tension for both readers and characters. On the one hand, it is what must be transcended by Maggie if she is to rise above "the mental level of the generation before" her. On the other, she is tied to that generation "by the strongest fibres of" her heart. In "the onward tendency of human things" the Dodsons and Tullivers must go, but they cannot be ignored and they must, indeed, be loved (see bk. 4, chap. 1).

The notions explicit in this view suggest how the story points to-wards both personal and social growth; and these notions are worked out in almost every detail of the novel. The town of St. Ogg's, to use only one example, has grown in a slow, incremental, entirely unplanned way. It has roots deep in the past, and every part of it is "familiar with forgotten years." Under the slow pressure of time the processes of cause and effect have built it, almost as a natural growth. And George Eliot certainly means to imply a parallel between social and natural law which is central to the beliefs we have been examining:

> It is one of those old, old towns which impress one as a con-
> tinuation and outgrowth of nature, as much as the nests of the
> bower-birds or the winding galleries of the white ants: a town
> which carries the traces of its long growth and history like a
> millennial tree, and has sprung up and developed in the same
> spot between the river and the low hill from the time when

the Roman legions turned their backs on it from the camp on
the hillside, and the long-haired sea-kings came up the river
and looked with fierce eager eyes at the fatness of the land.

(bk. 1, chap. 12)

Even the architecture suggests the natural connections with the primitive
sea-kings; equally, the citizens of St. Ogg's are what they are because of
the past: inconsistent, old-fashioned, egocentric, crude, but sympathetic
because they inherit—even without being aware of it—the best (along
with the worst) of what men have thought and felt. But because they
lack the clarity of vision Feuerbach desiderated they are determined: they
"inherited a long past without thinking of it" (bk. 1, chap. 12).

The Dodsons and Tullivers, of course, are the dramatic embodi-
ments of the town's essential nature, and they confirm the notion that
for George Eliot determinism is both dangerous and morally essential.
She saw with Feuerbach that society included not merely rigid conventions but also the slowly, painfully earned developments in man's intelligence and sensibility. Maggie, then, must learn what other characters
suffer by not learning—that everything must be judged on its unique
merits, that no laws, habits, or traditions can apply indiscriminately in
all situations. On the other hand, much of what she does learn in this
way turns out to be a "relearning" of the values already implicit in social
conventions. The trouble with the Dodsons and Tullivers is that they fail
to establish an adequate relation to their own traditions and are therefore
unable to understand their own motives derived from myriad causes out
of the past. Neither they nor Maggie quite attain the "objectivity" Feuerbach requires, the ability, that is, to see "the real relation of things."
They cannot achieve that "right understanding" of "the unchangeable
Order of the world" which Comte says "is the principal object of our
actions."

The predominant theme of the novel then, as George Eliot makes
explicit, is the quest for unity—social, familial, and personal—that fusion
of imagination and will which leads to sympathetic action. A convenient
summary of Feuerbach's views will suggest the direction George Eliot
wants Maggie's history to take:

The individual who has a strongly sympathetic nature combined with profound experience and the ability to imagine the
inner states of others has a moral life that is independent of
traditions; he has a more highly developed conscience and a
truer sense of good and evil than tradition, in its present state

of development, could supply. The sympathetic tendencies can lead a person to rebel against the harsh usages of tradition, even when such rebellion involves great personal risk.

But this combination of qualities, which can lead justifiably to a rebellion against convention, was more George Eliot's than Maggie's. It would not be stretching things to consider the possibility that these views of Feuerbach helped George Eliot justify to herself her decision to live with G. H. Lewes. But Maggie needs yet to unify her desires with her intentions, to discipline her passions in keeping with an objective view of possibility— "knowledge of the irreversible laws within and without her, which, governing the habits, becomes morality, and developing the feelings of submission and dependence, becomes religion" (bk. 4, chap. 3).

Socially, the quest is for unity between public opinion and individual sensibility. Comte places heavy emphasis on the value of public opinion in a way relevant to *The Mill on the Floss.* "The principal feature of the state to which we are tending," he says, "will be the increased influence which Public Opinion is destined to exercise. It is in this beneficial influence that we shall find the surest guarantee for morality. . . . Except the noblest of joys, that which springs from social sympathy when called into constant exercise, there is no reward for doing right so satisfactory as the approval of our fellow-beings." Maggie's relation to public opinion seems different, but that is partially because the society in which she lives is at such a primitive stage of development. George Eliot is certainly suggesting in the final chapters both the power of public opinion and the need to develop it more consistently to a higher level of social sympathy. The society of St. Ogg's, however, is disintegrating, as Dr. Kenn says, under the pressure of modern life, "seems tending toward the relaxation of ties—towards the substitution of wayward choice for adherence to obligation, which has its roots in the past" (bk. 7, chap. 1).

All aspects of the theme of unity are worked out in three of Maggie's moments of choice: her interview with Philip Wakem in the Red Deeps, her rowing party with Stephen Guest, and her refusal to stay with Stephen after they arrive at Mudport. The two earlier decisions show that Maggie has not achieved that personal unity which is essential to moral well-being. Philip is obviously right when, attacking her newfound asceticism, he warns her that if she persists in mere negations she will find that when she is "thrown upon the world . . . every rational satisfaction of your nature that you deny now, will assault you like a savage appetite" (bk. 5, chap. 3). Unfortunately, of course, even this sensible argument serves to weaken Maggie because it is not disinterested, but designed to keep her from leaving Philip altogether. The truth in this case is a lie, and deceit in the complicated deterministic universe of George Eliot is a form of moral disease whose dangers are far-reaching. It may be, as Maggie recognizes, that "it is other people's wrong feelings that make concealment necessary; but concealment is bad, however it may be caused" (bk. 5, chap. 3).

Nor has Maggie achieved unity by the time she meets Stephen Guest. Whatever one's objections to Stephen as a character, it is obvious that here as elsewhere George Eliot has been extremely careful to work out the reason for the action. What Maggie does with Stephen is determined by a past in which egotism and personal wilfulness keep her from moral integrity. There is no need here to list all the causes, but it is interesting to note how down to the finest details it is possible to observe kinship with the thought of Feuerbach and Comte. One of the things, for instance, which attracts Maggie to Stephen is his singing, and Maggie is deeply susceptible to music. Feuerbach argues strongly for the power of music: "What would man be without feeling?" he asks. "It is the musical power in man. But what would man be without music? Just as man has a musical faculty and feels an inward necessity to breathe out his feelings in song; so, by a like necessity, he, in religious sighs and tears, streams forth the nature of feeling as an objective, divine nature." Music, George Eliot remarks, "could hardly be without some intoxicating effect on her, after years of privation." It should be noted also that Maggie's desperate need to be admired and loved, one of the causes of her fall, corresponds closely to Comte's sense of what makes people behave as they do.

Because Maggie succumbs at her second moment of choice with Stephen, she is faced with a dilemma which is, in some ways, the purest in all of George Eliot's novels. Maggie's decision now cannot be in passive accordance with the push of circumstance; it depends on her understanding of the particular situation and cannot be governed by conventions. Simply by following out the implications of her complex attitudes towards tradition and modernity, self-control and self-assertion, George Eliot here arrives at a point where tradition cannot supply an adequate answer but where her heroine's character is inadequate to the task of Feuerbach's sympathetic rebellion. Maggie cannot even decide on the basis of the likely consequences of her actions because the damage has already been done and misery will be the consequence of either choice.

Thus, in making this third choice, Maggie achieves the highest level of consciousness of which a St. Ogg's citizen is capable. She reveals an awareness of the "real relation of things" by accepting both the irrevocability of her act and the fact that it "must blot her life" and bring sorrow into lives that were "knit up with hers by trust and love." She is aware that she has broken all "the ties that had given meaning to duty, and had made herself an outlawed soul," having lost the relation to community which, in Comte's sense, provides moral guidance; she was left with "no guide but the wayward choice of her own soul" (bk. 6, chap. 14). Recognizing this loss and its dangers, Maggie attempts to turn to the past and inherited traditions. "If the past is not to bind us," she says to Stephen, "where can duty lie: We have not law but the inclination of the moment" (bk. 6, chap. 14). Through the past she attempts to overcome the persistent fragmentation of self which has hitherto left her vulnerable to the past's uncomprehended forces.

She struggles against committing herself to a "momentary triumph of my feeling," to an evil which will form a habit of surrender to impulse and fragmentation. One of George Eliot's primary insights, dramatized in the curious passivity of her characters at their moments of choice, is that "character" as it has been formed over a lifetime finally determines how one will behave in a crisis. Untrained will is unequal to the pressures of the moment; the training of the will into a habit of goodness is essential because "moral behavior is only to be found in the spontaneous exercise of moral emotion. Moral action is not the result of a decision to act morally; it is the result of moral feeling, forcing itself into practice." At her present stage of development, Maggie must still labor at her choice, but she does move towards the unity of self which makes moral action a habit by recognizing that mind, memories, obligations are all part of what a man is, fully as important as natural feelings; and she tries to bring her feelings into conformity with her conscious intentions. The renunciation of Stephen moves one step beyond her immature asceticism, not based on a sense of the real relation of things, which Philip had criticized in the Red Deeps.

III

In keeping with her deterministic insistence on the pressure of ordinary events, her Comtean awareness of the moral pressures of public opinion, and the deep psychological perceptions she shared with Feuerbach about the nature of human suffering and morality, George Eliot could not allow Maggie's resolution yet to be final. Resolutions must be tested moment by moment and day by day and they must establish themselves in relation not only to the complete self but to the community. Thus, all the influences so carefully prepared through the apparently leisurely movement of the early stages of the novel come into play in the last book.

The tensions between the Dodsons and the Tullivers—between the two modes of egoism represented by the forces of convention uncomprehended and rigidified and the forces of blind spontaneity of feeling— now become in a more complex way the tensions between Maggie and the town. All of Maggie's past—not understood—contributed to her fatal lapse with Stephen; so all of Maggie's past—now largely if incompletely understood—contributes to her decision to return to St. Ogg's. Equally, all the seemingly innocuous circumstances which precede Maggie's lapse help determine the rigidly conventional—that is, unimaginative and therefore unsympathetic—response of the townspeople to Maggie. In language which suggests the quite conscious influence of both Comte and Feuerbach, George Eliot describes the "ladies of St. Ogg's" as "not beguiled by any wide speculative conceptions; but they had their favourite abstraction called society which seemed to make their consciences perfectly easy in doing what satisfied their egoism" (bk. 7, chap. 4). George Eliot's revulsion from abstractions is widely known, and in its temperamental character it is much more akin to Feuerbach than to Comte, who, though he insisted always on the positive and scientific, was himself the victim of abstractions. But this passage certainly evokes Comte, who, according to John Stuart Mill, described the "Metaphysical Stage" of human development as the stage which "accounts for phenomena by ascribing them, not to volitions either sublunary or celestial, but to realized abstractions. In this stage it is no longer a god that causes and directs each of the various agencies of nature: it is a power, or a force, or an occult quality, considered as real existence, inherent in but distinct from concrete bodies in which they reside, and which they in a manner animate."

The traditions animating the kind of Dodsonian behavior which condemns Maggie are given new life and meaning by the eldest of the Dodsons, Mrs. Glegg, who is capable of dealing with new kinds of experience because she is the strongest willed and most intelligent of the clan. Her willingness to oppose public opinion and convention is certainly intended as at least in part a dramatization of the way in which family unity—recognized by both Comte and Feuerbach as the source of morality—is the first step toward community, the first means of transcending the "I" for the "Thou," for breaking away from the narrow egoism which governs the action of ordinary men. It is the source of Maggie's higher sensibility, and as it is revivified in Mrs. Glegg it helps us to understand George Eliot's commitment to the sustaining power of tradition.

Despite Mrs. Glegg's help, however, the pressures on Maggie become strong enough to make her feel again the temptation to return to Stephen. She must once again work out the relation between self-will and self-denial, and George Eliot's comment on the problem reveals the impasse at which both author and heroine have arrived: "The great problem of the shifting relation between passion and duty is clear to no man who is capable of apprehending it: the question whether the moment has come in which a man has fallen below the possibility of a renunciation that will carry any efficacy, and must accept the sway of passion against which he had struggled as a trespass, is one for which we have no master-key that will fit all cases" (bk. 7, chap. 2). As the book has demonstrated, only in a society where egoism and self-will are not driven as in Maggie's case into excessive self-denial or, as in Tom's case, into respectability and moral brutality, does the problem of the shifting relation have a chance to be resolved. But such a positivist utopia, in which the individual and society are allied in one will, was, as George Eliot knew, a mere dream of the future, and one could only move towards it through the slow increment of wasted lives, of suffering such as Maggie's and Dorothea Brooke's, from which new moral insight can be assimilated into man's consciousness. Maggie is at an impasse which everything in the book has suggested is unresolvable. And Dr. Kenn's comment that any action she might take would be "clogged with evil" is undeniably true.

IV

The continuity of George Eliot's views is suggested by the similarity between Maggie's conflict as she battles temptation in the dark night preceding the flood and that of Dorothea on the night she resolves to accept Casaubon's unexplained demands. Both characters submit themselves to the higher responsibility despite the loss of the possibility of self-fulfillment. But neither character is made to face the full implications of such renunciation. Certainly, Dorothea does not achieve a fate with Ladislaw equal to her own large possibilities. Moreover, George Eliot means us to understand that her marriage to him will evoke considerable public disapprobation. But she is certainly not at such a primitive stage of development as Maggie, and Casaubon's death does save her from total and pointless frustration. This death follows almost immediately after her resolution, just as Maggie's death follows her own final renunciation.

In her first spontaneously moral action, she rushes to Tom's rescue and is swept to death in his arms, as though one were meant to see in that death her reconciliation to all those forces to which she could by temperament and action never be reconciled. Maggie's final action, however, can be seen as the last stage in the progress of her growth according to Feuerbach's principle and therefore altogether consistent with what has gone before. Beginning in mere egoism and rebellion, she moves on to the incomplete sympathy—as a result of family pressures—of her asceticism; the suffering which she endures intensifies that sympathy and produces in her a surer vision of reality so as to make her capable of a deliberate act of renunciation with Stephen; her rescue of Tom, however, is to be seen as a spontaneous moral action which suggests the real beginning of Feuerbach's genuinely noble man. But Maggie's newly earned "nobility" is once again exercised in the direction of her family, and will, moreover, never be tested in that infinitely more complicated social world which posed her moral dilemma. The escape, then, is thematically consistent, but it can be seen also as external and fortuitous, an intrusion of that "Favourable Chance" which George Eliot anathematized in *Silas Marner* (chap. 9).

One can only speculate on the reasons for such a lapse, characteristic not only of George Eliot's work but of much of the best work of the time. Perhaps Matthew Arnold's explanation of why he removed "Empedocles on Etna" from his 1853 *Poems* will throw light on the problem. Arnold, it will be remembered, asked with Schiller for an art "dedicated to Joy," since "there is no higher and more serious problem, than how to make men happy." George Eliot, for her part, during the decade following *The Mill on the Floss,* wrote that "the art which leaves the soul in despair is laming to the soul, and is denounced by the healthy sentiment of an active community." She is likely to have agreed with Arnold that there were certain situations, "from the representation of which, though accurate, no poetical enjoyment can be derived. They are those in which the suffering finds no vent in action; in which a continuous state of mental distress is prolonged, unrelieved by incident, hope, or resistance; in which there is everything to be endured, nothing to be done." This is Maggie's condition before the flood.

For Arnold, the solution was to abandon art for criticism; George

Eliot, also too intelligent and too responsible to let need consciously dictate to art, allowed herself to flaw her art, I would suggest, by deceiving herself with her own intelligence. She could, consistently with her own view of experience, avoid the condition Arnold described by leaning on Comte and Feuerbach; and in this way she could give Maggie the heroic, tragic, but largely affirmative action with which she dies. This action is consistent not only with the details of the plot as she carefully worked them out, but with the very themes which give the novel so much of its richness.

Moreover, within the system of Feuerbachian thought, the death by water makes good symbolic sense. Water, for Feuerbach, is one of the two major sacraments, the other and more important one being the bread and wine of the Lord's Supper. But although, as has been shown, much symbolic use of this sacrament occurs in *Adam Bede* there is apparently no such use in *The Mill on the Floss*. The crucial dinner scene in the first book marks not harmony but the beginning of the division between the Tullivers and Dodsons. The reason seems to be that *The Mill on the Floss* concerns itself with people on "a lower level generally"—not "lower" in class but in the development of their moral perceptions—with a society not prepared for the higher sacrament. Indeed, it is likely that George Eliot sees Maggie's death by water as a preparation for the condition in which the society would be prepared.

Water, for Feuerbach, is the sacrament which symbolically asserts man's dependence on nature; the flood serves to remind man of this. Curiously, in water "the scales fall from [man's] eyes: he sees and thinks more clearly," and at the same time "human mental activity is nullified." Both these effects of water operate in *The Mill on the Floss*. With Stephen Maggie falls into oblivion as she floats downstream; by contrast, with Tom the scales fall from her eyes as she reflects: "what quarrel, what harshness, what unbelief in each other can subsist in the presence of a great calamity, when all the artificial vesture of our life is gone, and we are all one with each other in primitive mortal needs" (bk. 7, chap. 5). Here, appropriately, Maggie not only "sees and thinks more clearly," but she is forced to these reflections by the power of Nature over the merely "artificial." And, of course, in the death which follows, consciousness is nullified, but only after, by symbolically crying "Maggie," Tom avers the love which dominated in the natural state of childhood. The death is a purification of both Maggie and Tom: "To purify oneself," as Feuerbach says, "to bathe, is the first, though the lowest of virtues."

This, it seems to me, is George Eliot's attitude towards the final catastrophe; Tom and Maggie must achieve "the first, though the lowest of virtues" because even now neither they nor St. Ogg's is ready for the higher, active, creative virtues of man's full consciousness and power.

One more quotation from Feuerbach should suggest other ways in which the conclusion of *The Mill on the Floss* was firmly a part of the intellectual structure of the book: "It needs only that the ordinary course of things be interrupted in order to vindicate to common things an uncommon significance, *to life, as such, a religious import.* Therefore let bread be sacred for us, let wine be sacred, and also let water be sacred! Amen." For George Eliot, the inability to see the extraordinariness of the ordinary is an aspect of that egoism and lack of imagination which characterizes the society of St. Ogg's. She insists on the religious import, surely in Feuerbach's sense, of the ordinary, and thus follows Feuerbach by introducing into the novel the extraordinary—the flood—which is in fact only an extreme development of the ordinary and which in its extreme quality takes on the nature of a ritual. It is curious how so many of George Eliot's novels, however much the great bulk of events they include are assertively ordinary, turn on events which seem to come directly out of melodrama—Arthur Donnithorne's last-minute rescue of Hetty, the final meeting of Baldassarre and Tito, Grandcourt's drowning and Mordecai's mystical Zionist visions, the revelation of Transome's relation to the lawyer Jermyn.

It is perhaps too simple to suggest that this sort of refusal to face the total implication of her own ideas and of her very temperament was the result of George Eliot's conscious effort to protect "her readers from any 'laming' effects." Obviously George Eliot did seek moral order in the bleakest and most amoral elements of the world. But she was too intelligent to be satisfied with emotional need unsustained by intellectual conviction. Feuerbach, at least in *The Mill on the Floss,* seems to have supplied her with an intellectually satisfying and emotionally acceptable answer. Because we take George Eliot's perceptions to the point of the modern vision, where the only affirmation is personal, inward, and isolated, we tend to believe that in honesty she needed to do the same thing. But she turns away with characteristic Victorian strength and integrity in search of meaning, justice, and the organic community. We could do much worse.

Tragedy and the Flux:
The Mill on the Floss

U. C. Knoepflmacher

The Mill on the Floss is divided into seven books, which can be separated into two movements: in the first, Mr. Tulliver, like Amos Barton, vainly tries to shore his present against the impending future; in the second, where that future becomes the present of his children, Tom and Maggie vainly try to recover their childhood at Dorlcote Mill. The first movement concludes with Mr. Tulliver's death at the end of book 5; the second culminates with the drowning of Tom and Maggie. Like *Antony and Cleopatra,* the novel thus contains two related tragedies, which I shall examine individually only for the sake of making critical distinctions. In Shakespeare's play, Cleopatra's sacrifice is meant to exalt Antony's bungling death; in her tragic novel, George Eliot likewise intends Maggie's sacrifice to lend a wider meaning to the little world ignobly lost through Mr. Tulliver's recklessness. The miller's gradual ruin and self-destruction are deftly handled by a novelist sure of her control. The rash miller is in his way as convincing a tragic figure as the impetuous Antony. But George Eliot could not handle Maggie's fate with the same assurance. For reasons which I shall examine in the last section of this chapter, George Eliot failed to convert Maggie's immolation into an action as world-stirring as that of Shakespeare's Cleopatra.

Mr. Tulliver's story introduces all the basic collisions of the novel:

From *George Eliot's Early Novels: The Limits of Realism.* © 1968 by the Regents of the University of California. University of California Press, 1968.

the antithesis between the worlds of the Mill by the Ripple and of St. Ogg's-on-the-Floss, the contrast between Dodsons and Tullivers, the resulting oppositions between parents and children, brother and sister, and Maggie's consequent self-division. Yet the unit which ends with the miller's deathbed recognition that the "world's been too many" for him, possesses the tragic requisites which the remainder of the novel lacks. Like Oedipus, to whom he is compared by the narrator, Mr. Tulliver has become entangled in "the skein of life" through his own blind pride. Unlike the symbolic flood which executes Tom and Maggie, the catastrophe which marks his downfall is the direct result of the interaction of character and destiny, will and fate. Mr. Tulliver falls victim to his own faulty choices. He first selects a spouse for her presumed submissiveness and stupidity; then, betrayed by the unexpected biological "crossing o' breeds," he prefers his Tulliver daughter over his Dodson son. To prepare for Tom's future, he chooses a "gentleman's" education which is as unprofitable as that of Amos Barton or Dickens's Pip; he adopts the advice of Mr. Riley instead of enlisting the better judgment of Mr. Deane, his brother-in-law, whom he regards as "the 'knowingest' man of his acquaintance," but whom he does not consult on family matters because of vanity and pride. Able to avoid a costly litigation, the imprudent miller opts a lawsuit instead and thus finally places himself in the power of Chancery, that Victorian embodiment of ancient "Fortuna." Incapable of adapting to the changes taking place around him, he escapes, as Maggie will, into rebellion, fantasy, and, eventually, death. Unlike his daughter, however, he is far more the victim of his own hubris than of capricious chance.

Mr. Deane is the miller's exact counterpart. A self-made city man, he knows the ways of the world. The foolish Mr. Tulliver congratulates himself for having chosen a classicist as Tom's teacher. Always impulsive, he soon convinces himself that the boy's tutor is a "clergyman whose knowledge was so applicable to the everyday affairs of this life. Except Counsellor Wylde, whom he had heard at the last session, Mr. Tulliver thought the Rev. Mr. Stelling was the shrewdest fellow he had ever met with—not unlike Wylde, in fact: he had the same way of sticking his thumbs in the armholes of his waistcoat" (bk. 2, chap. 1). The utilitarian Mr. Deane, on the other hand, soon brands Tom's education as utterly useless. Even after the youth pathetically promises to unlearn his Latin and ancient history, Mr. Deane presses on contemptuously: "Your Latin and rigmarole may soon dry off you, but you'll be but a bare stick after that. Besides, it's whitened your hands and taken the rough work out of you. And what do you know? Why, you know nothing about book-keeping, to begin with, and not so much of reckoning as a common shopman. You'll have to begin at the low round of the ladder, let me tell you, if you mean to get on in life. It's no use forgetting the education your father's been paying for, if you don't give yourself a new un" (bk. 3, chap. 5). Ironically, the very man whose advice Mr. Tulliver shunned, now teaches his Dodson son how to repair the father's mistakes.

Mr. Deane typifies the new ways of St. Ogg's. Like Lawyer Wakem, he plays Octavius to Mr. Tulliver's Antony. The miller who gallops incessantly around his threatened land is impulsive and sentimental; his unlanded brother-in-law exerts himself only by "taking snuff vigorously, as he always did when wishing to maintain a neutral position" (bk. 1, chap. 7). Like Wakem, Mr. Deane remains evasive and noncommittal. Whereas Mr. Tulliver identifies his archenemy with "old Harry" himself, Mr. Deane cautiously respects Lawyer Wakem as a powerful business rival. Mr. Tulliver vows that he will not allow "anybody get hold of his whip-hand" (bk. 1, chap. 5), but when he loses control of his lands, it is his brother-in-law who asks the stricken miller to accept Wakem's demeaning offer to let him manage the property he formerly owned. Mr. Deane could easily have outbid the lawyer in order to salvage Mr. Tulliver's pride, but he does not "carry on business on sentimental grounds" (bk. 3, chap. 7). In his unromantic world a man can succeed only by waiting patiently, as he has done, "before he got the whip in his hand" (bk. 6, chap. 5). If the descendant of the fiery Ralph Tulliver rides against the times, his prudent counterpart moves with the tide. Once regarded as the worst match made by the Dodson sisters, Mr. Deane has gradually risen to eminence in the Guests' "great mill-owning, ship-owning business." Progress is his motto as much as it is that of Dickens's Podsnap or Gradgrind: "I don't find fault with the change, as some people do. Trade, sir, opens a man's eyes; and if population is to get thicker upon the ground, as it's doing, the world must use its wits at inventions of some sort or other" (bk. 6, chap. 5).

While Mr. Tulliver loses control of his mill wheel by entering useless litigations over his decreasing "water-power," the self-controlled Mr. Deane steadily gains in influence by harnessing new sources of power: "It's this steam, you see, that has made the difference: it drives on every wheel double pace, and the wheel of fortune along with 'em, as our Mr. Stephen Guest said" (bk. 6, chap. 5). If Mr. Tulliver is the enfeebled survivor of Carlyle's "Heroical Age," Mr. Deane belongs to the new mechanical era "which, with its whole undivided might, forwards, teaches, and practices the great art of adapting means to ends." Deane's sphere of action seems every bit as removed from Dorlcote Mill as Caesar's Rome is from Cleopatra's Egypt. At the mill, the relation between Luke and his master still resembles that of a vassal and his feudal lord; Luke's loyalty is not unlike the devotion of a Kent or Enobarbus. For the world soon to be lost by the miller is archaic enough to harbor what Hegel had called "romantic fidelity." In it the ideal of service remains as untouched as the urge for revenge which dominates the "pagan" Mr. Tulliver and his son. Like old Adam in *As You Like It,* Luke wants to give his earnings to his master, for he feels, "after the manner of contented hard-working men whose lives have been spent in servitude, that sense of natural fitness in rank which made his master's downfall a tragedy to him" (bk. 3, chap. 8).

In St. Ogg's no such "natural fitness" exists. Luke and his master are equals despite the difference in rank; but Mr. Deane and Lawyer Wakem head a society in which mastery can be established only by competition and strife. Mr. Deane will not try to outbid Lawyer Wakem; he cannot afford to be ruled by sentiments such as Luke's. Tom, on the other hand, immediately on accepting the responsibilities of his father's position, decides to pay Luke, "if in no other way, out of his own and Maggie's money." In *As You Like It,* freed by old Adam's money, Orlando and his father's servant jointly escape into the Forest of Arden. In George Eliot's novel, there is no sanctuary. Luke's refusal to accept the payment due him cannot free either him or his young master. Tom must go to St. Ogg's to restore his father's good name. The irony is bitter. Simply by walking across the "stone bridge" that leads into the city he enters a different world. Before crossing that bridge, Tom still looked at reality with his father's eyes: "he saw the distant future before him, as he might have seen a tempting stretch of smooth sandy beach beyond a belt of flinty shingles; he was on the grassy bank then, and thought the shingles might soon be passed." But he returns as Mr. Deane's disciple: "now his feet were on the sharp stones; the belt of shingles had widened, and the stretch of sand had dwindled into narrowness" (bk. 3, chap. 5). His vision has been adjusted. To fight Lawyer Wakem he has submitted to Wakem's oppressive world.

Like Lawyer Dempster before him, Wakem is identified with the devil himself. Although the association is made by the superstitious Mr. Tulliver, there is a tinge of truth to it. For even more than Dempster's Milby, St. Ogg's is a modern equivalent of the "city of destruction" from which Bunyan's Christian had escaped. In Milby, Mr. Tryan had been able to rescue Janet Dempster from damnation and despair; in St. Ogg's, no such Evangelist can rescue the modern pilgrim. Even the kindhearted Dr. Kenn must yield to the pressure of his parishioners and evict Maggie from his house. The historical past of St. Ogg's only confirms the nature of its present. Like the Rome described in *Middlemarch,* the city is merely an aggregate of historical strata, each of which has stifled and suppressed the one beneath it. In "The Lifted Veil," Latimer had seen one such layer in his vision of Prague. Here, the narrator mercilessly uncovers all the calcified deposits of the past. The intermittent floods have only separated one age of strife from another. The present warehouses of Guest & Co. rest on the site of struggle far bloodier than those of industrial competition. Only less than two centuries ago, the town had witnessed "worse troubles even than the floods—troubles of the civil wars, when it was a continual fighting-place, where first Puritans thanked God for the blood of the Loyalists, and then Loyalists thanked God for the blood of the Puritans" (bk. 1, chap. 12). Digging deeper, the narrator unearths further collisions: the era of the church displaced the invasion of the Norman conquerors; the Danish raiders overcame the Saxon settlers; the Vikings ended the predominance of the Roman legions. Even in the days of St. Ogg, the son of Beorl, hardhearted and indifferent men repulsed the sufferer he ferried across the river. In the city's present historical phase, where religion has given way to politics, only one superannuated inhabitant still recollects having heard that same John Wesley whose words Dinah Morris had carried into Loamshire's green pastoral land.

If Mr. Tulliver's latter-day agrarian existence is threatened by the industrial present of St. Ogg's, his defeat is not as inevitable as it would be in a dialectic Marxist view. For George Eliot carefully contrasts the miller's failures with the success of the Dodsons. Both families are equally archaic in their "pagan" clannishness and social orientation. Yet while Mr. Tulliver and his only sister, Mrs. Moss, find their strength depleted, the Dodsons manage to conserve their power. Once regarded as the "buck of Basset," Mr. Moss, Gritty Tulliver's husband, has become a dehumanized "machine-horse"; his farm yields diminishing returns. The husbands of the Dodson sisters, however, have all added to their wives' dowries. Like Dickens's Wemmick, both the landed Mr. Pullet and the unlanded Mr. Glegg understand the value of "portable property." If Mr. Tulliver's aggressiveness is ineffectual, their defensive tactics prove to be invincible. The Gleggs have even moved into the enemy citadel, St. Ogg's itself. Financially secure as a moneylender, Mr. Glegg can, like Wemmick, that other amiable Harpagon, easily transfer the country into the town. Contentedly, he follows his farming instincts by cultivating his back yard. His house affords two vistas, "two points of view." It faces the busy world of St. Ogg's and the road which leads out of the city into Tofton, the suburb where both Mr. Deane and Lawyer Wakem have built handsome houses (building materials dislodged from Tofton's wharves will kill Tom and Maggie). The back windows reveal a more idyllic scene, "the pleasant garden and orchard which stretched to the river" (bk. 1, chap. 12). In that makeshift Eden, Mr. Glegg can relax by doing "the work of two ordinary gardeners." While his brother-in-law Mr. Deane exploits the river, Mr. Glegg enjoys its shores and remains unaffected by its motions.

Tragedy cannot touch Mr. Glegg. He picked the eldest Miss Dodson as a "handsome embodiment of female prudence and thrift." His choice of a partner is made after his own image: "being himself of a money-getting, money-keeping turn, [he] had calculated on much conjugal harmony" (bk. 1, chap. 12). As always in George Eliot's fiction, his "calkilations" are not wholly correct. But though Mrs. Glegg is somewhat of a shrew, she does not really impede her husband's well-being. Mr. Tulliver, on the other hand, must very definitely pay for having picked a wife so unlike himself. He chose Elizabeth Dodson, he smugly informs Mr. Riley, because "she was a bit weak, like; for I wasn't agoin' to be told the rights o' things by my own fireside" (bk. 1, chap. 3). Like Lydgate in *Middlemarch,* Mr. Tulliver should not have dabbled in natural selection. For not only does his choice result in the unforeseen Mendelian "crossing" which gives Maggie her father's characteristics and endows Tom with those of the Dodsons, but it also contributes directly to his own downfall.

As an "amiable hen" who usually defers to her husband, children, and sisters, Mrs. Tulliver resembles Mrs. Bennet rather than Antony's Cleopatra. Nonetheless, her husband's tragic fate is tied to the rudder of his chosen queen. Passive as she is, Mrs. Tulliver's few actions always have an effect opposite from that which she intends. Although she knows that her splenetic husband will be incensed by any opinion contrary to his own, she dutifully invites all her sisters and their husbands to discuss Tom's education—even though the miller has already made a decision. The meeting sets in motion the sequence of events which will lead to the loss of Dorlcote Mill. Angered by Mrs. Glegg's criticism, Mr. Tulliver vows to pay back the five hundred pounds she had loaned him. His wife's attempts to mediate only rankle his pride. Even though he also is in debt to Mr. Furley, the miller insists on returning the money to his sister-in-law at once. But by refusing to be indebted to Mrs. Glegg or Mrs. Pullet, this Chanticleer closes his eyes and only places himself a step closer to the fox. Against his will or better judgment, Mr. Tulliver becomes bonded to one of Lawyer Wakem's clients: "'It must be no client of Wakem's,' he said to himself; and yet at the end of a fortnight it turned out to the contrary; not because Mr. Tulliver's will was feeble, but because external fact was stronger. Wakem's client was the only convenient person to be found. Mr. Tulliver had a destiny as well as Œdipus, and in this case he might plead, like Œdipus, that his deed was inflicted on him rather than committed by him" (bk. 1, chap. 13).

But Mr. Tulliver's mate contributes still further to his self-inflicted "destiny." After the miller loses a lawsuit in which he has foolishly supposed that he can best Lawyer Wakem on the lawyer's own terrain, his henlike wife takes up her husband's cause by making a foray into the enemy camp. But her undiplomatic efforts to dissuade Wakem from bidding for her husband's land only put a new thought into the shrewd lawyer's mind. Before her visit, he had no intention of bidding against Mr. Deane. Now, however, he decides on the very course of action she had set out to prevent. Although George Eliot probes into the lawyer's motives, she also suggests that he is only an agent for the fate brought on by the miller's own rashness. If Octavius is too cold-blooded to hate his hot-tempered rival, Wakem is no more guilty of wrath "than an ingenious machine, which performs its work with much regularity, is guilty towards the rash man who, venturing too near it, is caught up by some fly-wheel or other, and suddenly converted into unexpected mince-meat" (bk. 3, chap. 7). After flogging one of Octavius's messengers, Antony whips himself into a frenzy and wins a land battle against the enemy who had defeated him by water. Mistaking a minor skirmish for a major triumph, Antony is soon driven to suicide. Mr. Tulliver also wins a minor engagement when he repays his creditors through the efforts of his son. Yet foolishly flushed by his success, he dies of apoplexy after flogging Wakem with his whip. The lawyer escapes with a sprained arm. Like Antony, the romantic Mr. Tulliver has even bungled his exit from life.

In an essay entitled "Tragedy and the Common Man," Arthur Miller once argued that the terror and fear of tragedy could still be evoked in a modern everyman's exposure to the pressures of social change. Defending *Death of a Salesman,* the playwright contended: "I believe that the common man is as apt a subject for tragedy in its highest sense as kings were." To the reader of *The Mill on the Floss,* the statement carries a somewhat familiar ring:

> Mr. Tulliver, you perceive, though nothing more than a superior miller and maltster, was as proud and obstinate as if he had been a very lofty personage, in whom such dispositions might be a source of that conspicuous, far-echoing tragedy, which sweeps the stage in regal robes, and makes the dullest chronicler sublime. The pride and obstinacy of millers, and other insignificant people, whom you pass unnoticingly on the road every day, have their tragedy too.
>
> (bk. 3, chap. 1)

But George Eliot's superior miller is a much more tragic figure than Miller's Loman; there is more poetry in the loss of an ancestral mill than in an aging salesman's loss of his former "territory." Like Willy Loman, Mr. Tulliver, incapable of adjusting himself to the ways of the future, escapes into a dreamworld and ponders what might have been. But Willy's end is pathetic, whereas there is a magnificence in Mr. Tulliver's impenitent death. The miller who demands a "retributive justice" barely recognizes that he also must pay for his mistakes. Yet his nemesis does inspire us with the true terror of tragedy. The impersonal order which pushes him aside seems more fearsome than Willy's displacement by a boss who plays with a tape recorder. Willy smashes his car so that his wife and children can collect his insurance money; his death is a deliberate act by which he intends to repair the damage he has done. Mr. Tulliver's injuries to his family, however, cannot be repaired. His fall is more momentous. The indifference with which Mr. Deane and Mr. Glegg regard their brother-in-law's lost "water-power" is far closer, artistically, to the indifference which Goneril and Regan display toward Lear's regal attributes than it is to Howard's refusal to augment Willy Loman's Social Security payments. In the eyes of St. Ogg's, Mr. Tulliver is incompetent. In his archaic world, however, Maggie's fond and foolish father remains a "lofty personage." Accordingly, his fall is far more princely than that of the "hardworking, unappreciated prince" who is the father of the neurotic Biff.

Before dying, King Lear recognizes the goodness of the daughter he has so unjustly spurned; before his death, Mr. Tulliver must acknowledge his debt to the son he had tried to keep away from his own mill. He hopes that Tom will take care of the little "wench" who is the true bearer of his Tulliver blood. Yet, like Lear's kingdom or the "patrimonial fields" of Wordsworth's Michael, Dorlcote Mill is an heirloom that will go to no direct successors. Held by the Tullivers for "a hundred years and over," it will not be repossessed by the miller's descendants. Wordsworth's guiltless Michael loses lands that once were free like himself when his son Luke goes to the "dissolute city" and gives himself to "evil courses." Though they too must go to that city, neither Tom nor Maggie really fails their father. Yet they lack his freedom. Michael asks his son to reclaim the land which otherwise would not endure another master. Mr. Tulliver, on the other hand, dimly senses that the mill is lost forever. He tells his servant: "There's a story as when the mill changes hands, the river's angry—I've heard my father say it many a time" (bk. 3, chap. 9). His prophecy proves true. The angry river will claim his Dodson son and Tulliver daughter. Freedom of will gives way to accident and capricious forces. A different order of reality has taken over.

THE DISINURED PAST: THE SACRIFICE OF MAGGIE TULLIVER

The opening books of *The Mill on the Floss* contain some of George Eliot's finest writing. Comedy and tragedy are combined through the "negative capability" which Keats recognized in Shakespeare. Ironic, tough-minded, the novelist is capable of moving our deeper emotions without ever lapsing into sentimentality. The story of a superior miller and maltster contains analogues to the stories of Lear or Antony for the mind willing to connect the smaller to the greater. Yet though we sense Mr. Tulliver's greatness, we are never allowed to forget his limitations. High and low, heroic and mock-heroic, are held in perfect equipoise through the Victorian device of "inverse sublimity." It is therefore all the more shocking to watch this equipoise break down completely in the last volume of the novel (bks. 6 and 7). After Mr. Tulliver's death, Maggie displaces Tom on George Eliot's stage. The tiny girl of the earlier portions of the novel is now aggrandized into a "fallen princess" who is denied her regal robes by her unheroic inferiors. Conversely, the St. Ogg's which was so terrifying to the puzzled miller becomes shrunken, exposed in its full pettiness. From Shakespeare and Wordsworth we have moved to Pope: in the opening of book 6, Stephen Guest stands poised with a pair of scissors, ready to shear off one of Lucy's straying curls. Teacups, ratafias, a piano, have replaced the poetic Dorlcote Mill. The narrator's voice has lost its sureness, shifting uneasily between satire and sentimentalism with the same uncertainty that George Eliot had exhibited in "Amos Barton."

The narrator describes Stephen's dandified attire as "the graceful and odoriferous result of the largest oil-mill and the most extensive wharf in St. Ogg's" (bk. 6, chap. 1). He suggests sarcastically that there is only an "apparent triviality in the action of the scissors," hinting thereby that the actions of this young man (whose appearance in the book is so sudden and unexpected) are every bit as trivial as the activities of the society to which he owes his wealth. But the attempt to typify in Stephen the society headed by his father and by Mr. Deane, his prospective father-in-law, seems heavy-handed. The satire misfires rather badly, for it has the effect of reducing the scope of the very forces that had led to Mr. Tulliver's downfall. The clear-cut, all-too-explicit picture of the "small world" that stifles Maggie with its puerilities, can hardly disturb us as deeply as the more general picture of the impersonal flywheel which had vanquished her father. The disparity between the small and the great is no longer handled ironically. In the previous portions of the book the actions of Mr. Tulliver and of little Maggie, though insignificant, were prompted by the Μέγεθος [megethos] of true passion. But later not even so imposing an agent as a biblical flood can impress tragedy on the world of *The Rape of the Lock*. The machinery of Pope's mock-epic jars with that used in earnest by such nineteenth-century imitators of Milton as John Abraham Heraud in his twelve-book epic *The Judgement of the Flood* (1834). The small and the great have become arbitrarily reversed, as well as sundered.

Even before the opening of the novel's third volume, there is a marked shift in treatment and style. If Maggie the child and Mr. Tulliver were viewed by a narrator able to maintain an aesthetic distance, the young woman's story is writ "large" whenever she makes her appearance. Whereas the commonplace miller became an Œdipus only by a stretch of our imaginations, George Eliot now tries to assist us whenever possible by likening the miller's daughter to a "tall Hamadryad" whose "queenly head" is juxtaposed to a hastily introduced backdrop of "grand Scotch firs." The ideological skeleton of the novel, so superbly enfleshed in the first half of the narrative, shows increasingly through a veneer of skin. Only by implication was Mr. Tulliver a prince falling from high to low; Maggie, however, is actually described as a regal figure without the kneeling subjects she so richly deserves. The child who wanted to be crowned as queen of the gypsies, who invented a world in which Lucy was queen, "though the queen was Maggie herself in Lucy's form" (bk. 1, chap. 7), now must escape with Lucy's Prince Charming before discovering that he too is hopelessly unworthy of her. And we are not allowed to forget the "jet crown" upon this exquisite creature's head.

Though Maggie is presumably guilty of the Tulliver pride, she is made to seem far less culpable than her willful father. Mr. Tulliver's exchanges with his wife, her relatives, or Mr. Riley always revealed his own deficiencies. The adult Maggie's exchanges with Philip or Stephen Guest seem by comparison to be hollow recitations. When Philip tells her that he has "nothing but the past to live upon," and plaintively asks her whether "the future will never join on to the past again," Maggie answers in similar abstractions: "I desire no future that will break the ties of the past" (bk. 6, chap. 10). To Stephen's entreaties that she accept the future he offers her, Maggie replies: "You feel, as I do, that the real tie lies in the feelings and expectations we have raised in other minds. Else all pledges might be broken, when there was no outward penalty. There would be no such thing as faithfulness" (bk. 6, chap. 11). When, drifting down the river, she suddenly awakes to Duty and Memory, she proclaims: "If the past is not to bind us, where can duty lie? We should have no law but the inclination of the moment" (bk. 6, chap. 14). Such speeches belong to a thesis-novel. They ought to come from a ventriloquist's puppet and not from the rounded human being whose growth we have observed. George Eliot has dropped all indirection. She glosses Maggie's willingness to be led by Stephen in the boat with a laconic statement, "Memory was excluded," as if an explicit stage direction could substitute for what the reader ought to feel through his own experience. Yet Maggie must be readied to play out her role as victim or martyr.

Though pitiful, Mr. Tulliver was not spared the ironic treatment accorded to his rivals in St. Ogg's; the adult Maggie, however, is untouched by the sarcasm with which the author ridicules the pretensions of a society far more sterile than Milby. Pretending to adopt the voice of "not the world, but the world's wife" (bk. 7, chap. 2), the narrator becomes a satirist who blames society for barring its doors to an innocent victim. Maligned and defamed as Mr. Tryan had been, the "large-souled" Maggie becomes too precious for this world—even for the aunt who now surprises us by welcoming the young outcast. Life at the Ripple cannot be recovered. Rowing towards the Mill, Maggie notices a "rushing muddy current that must be the strangely altered Ripple" (bk. 7, chap. 5). Paradise has been washed away and soiled by the irresistible flux. Maggie must surrender. Only death can rescue the girl who demanded a higher life: in "dreadful clearness" she and Tom behold the "hurrying, threatening masses" which will engulf them in the river's current.

The concluding portions of *The Mill on the Floss* not only lack, in Professor Haight's words, "the same degree of realism" found in the earlier parts, but they also betray a severe loss of artistic control. Although George Eliot spent but nine weeks on the last two books of her novel, it is highly doubtful that more time and care might have made Maggie's tragedy seem more appropriate. Several reasons have been advanced for the unsatisfactory resolution of the novel. Of all the explanations, that offered by George Levine comes closest to the heart of the matter. To him, the conclusion indicates the novelist's need to "escape from the implications of her most deeply felt insights." Pulling back from the nihilism inherent in "modern sensibility," George Eliot was able to dignify the amoral and accidental existence she distrusted only by treating Maggie's death as an extraordinary martyrdom. Mr. Levine's argument seems generally cogent, even though he almost seems to blame George Eliot for not being William Faulkner. What is more, since he advances his thesis for all of George Eliot's fiction, it is his burden to show whether his conclusions apply equally to her other works. Indeed, his statement does not adequately explain why the author who had succeeded so admirably with Mr. Tulliver's tragedy should have failed in depicting Maggie's plight.

George Eliot's variation can be accounted for only if we carefully examine some of the difficulties she faced in relating Tom's and Maggie's stories to that of their father. That these difficulties had their origins in Marian Evans's need to define her own identity through her precarious relationship with both her father and brother, though undeniably true, need not concern us in this study of the novelist's more conscious intentions. (I leave it up to critics more versed in Freud to interpret the significance of the two dreams Maggie has before her "real waking" on Stephen's boat.) Both Tom and Maggie, we are told by the narrator, have evolved "above the mental level of the generation before them." In Tom, the Dodson strain has been magnified; in Maggie, the "richer blood" of the Tullivers is dominant (bk. 4, chap. 2). Though Tom has inherited his mother's literalism, his tenacity is even greater than that of the strongest of her sisters. Though Maggie possesses her father's faculty for perceiving that words can stand for "summat else," her greater imagination demands a more grandiose outlet for her unsatisfied intelligence and affection. Tom embraces the reality of St. Ogg's; Maggie yields to the fantasy life that was her father's destruction.

If Mr. Tulliver refused Mr. Deane's advice, Tom not only works for his uncle but also lets himself be guided by the practical Bob Jakin. Bob's strength, like Mr. Deane's, lies in his adaptability. Even as Tom's boyhood companion, he had boasted of his instinct for survival: "'*I* don't care about a flood comin',' said Bob; 'I don't mind the water, no more nor the land. I'd swim—*I* would.'" Like some of the organisms mentioned by the narrator, the amphibian Bob belongs to a species hardy enough to adapt himself to a change in environment. Aware that there is no future for him as a bargeman or rat-catcher, he chooses what to him is a less appealing profession. Bob prospers as a packman; Tom rises in his uncle's firm. Both turn their backs on a "paradisiac picture," determined to get on in the world. Yet Tom's fierce determination lacks Bob's warmth and humor. He has no time for such amenities as a wife and family. Tom's words shock even his uncle: "I want to have plenty of work. There's nothing else I care about much" (bk. 6, chap. 5). Transplanted to St. Ogg's, Adam Bede's doctrine of work seems grim and materialistic. In his monomaniac desire to recover Mr. Tulliver's mill Tom inherits only the miller's intolerance: "his inward criticism of his father's faults did not prevent him from adopting his father's prejudice" (bk. 6, chap. 12). In his desire to vindicate the past, he betrays all that was best in it by yielding uncritically to his present.

Maggie, on the other hand, cannot at all adapt herself to this changed present. As a child she fancied a world where people never got larger than the children of her own age. This fantasy sets her apart from Tom and links her to her father. The miller's incapacity to grow, his paranoid hostility toward the incomprehensible world that impinges on him, prefigures the predicament of his daughter. His maladjustment, however, is treated with an almost clinical objectivity. The novelist makes it clear that, like Mr. Toobad in Peacock's *Nightmare Abbey,* Mr. Tulliver blames his own irresponsibility on the machinations of the devil. But whereas she exposes the simplicity of the miller's evasions of reality, George Eliot cannot bring herself to do the same when she depicts his daughter's plight. Instead, significantly enough, the narrator now appropriates the miller's hostility against the world at large. If Mr. Tulliver foolishly blames "old Harry" for his own inability to find fulfillment, our intelligent narrator is forced to blame a different fiction—"the world's wife." In the second chapter of the last book, "St. Ogg's Passes Judgment," the narrator pauses to satirize this imaginary figure for maligning poor Maggie. The world's wife, he tells us, has its own favorite abstraction, called "society." Yet the narrator does not hesitate to vent his own spleen on this same abstraction. As Mr. Levine suggests, intelligence can often lead to self-deception; so, obviously, can emotion.

In "The Lifted Veil," the disabled Latimer helplessly awaited the moment of his death; in *The Mill on the Floss,* Mr. Tulliver watches the auctioning of all his belongings after he has been immobilized by a stroke, and Maggie and Tom stand paralyzed in their boat as they see "death rushing on them." All four characters are equally defenseless. Yet it is Maggie, rather than her masculine brother or father, who most resembles the passive and prostrate Latimer. Like the protagonist of George Eliot's horror tale, Maggie is choiceless, the victim of her creator's apprehension over the blind chance which may determine identity and fate. To an even greater extent than Latimer (who might have been saved by Meunier), Maggie is powerless to alter her fate. While George Eliot makes Mr. Tulliver seem blameworthy for his imprudence, she comes close to pretending that Maggie's destiny is absolutely sealed because predetermined by "the irreversible laws within and without her" (bk. 4, chap. 3).

The outside forces affecting Maggie are withstood by her brother by virtue of his Dodson tenacity; the inner forces weakening her come from the characteristics she has inherited from her father. Like Mr. Tulliver, the girl possesses a "soul untrained for inevitable struggles"; like the miller, she is deeply neurotic, incapable of accepting what Freud would call the "reality principle." Maggie therefore not only succumbs to the social changes which destroy her father, but she is also victimized by a trick of heredity, by the "crossing of breeds" by the miller who had perversely chosen a wife so unlike himself. Had Maggie, and not Tom, been a man, she might have profited from Mr. Stelling's education, gone on to the university, and become a "gentleman" like Pendennis or even a gentleman-novelist like Thackeray himself. Had she, instead of Tom, retained her mother's characteristics, or, better still, have remained at the "mental level" of Mrs. Tulliver, she might have become an ordinary governess in a world without Byronic Rochesters or Gothic manor houses, contentedly mangling her master's sheets instead of having the world mangle her psyche. But, by a hereditary caprice, Mr. Tulliver's favorite child is a throwback to the heroic Ralph Tulliver, and hence is all the more unfitted to cope with the world than her father. She may well wish to remain insignificant, to lead the untroubled life of a child, "easy and simple, as it might have been in Paradise" (bk. 6, chap. 11); but in George Eliot's deterministic view of existence, such regression is not only unhealthy but also impossible. In a simpler era when Tom could have been an Adam Bede, unseduced by the ways of St. Ogg's, Maggie might have become a Dinah embracing the "reality principle." But in her stage the chasm has become too wide. The reentry into a less troubled stage of life can come only through the return to those "daisied fields" which Tom and Maggie are allowed to revisit in the flash of time which elapses before their drowning. Though treated as a greater character than her father, Maggie seems infinitely punier because she is so irrevocably determined by his genes. Character may not be destiny, as the narrator warns us, but neither are chromosomes. As Ibsen was to discover later in the century, tragedy and heredity are difficult to mix.

Like the witch in the book she shows to Mr. Riley, Maggie is condemned, regardless of her choice. Whichever way she turns lies hell. The moral which this shrewd little girl derives from her book applies to her later self:

> O, I'll tell you what that means. It's a dreadful picture, isn't it? But I can't help looking at it. That old woman in the water's a witch—they've put her in to find out whether she's a witch or no, and if she swims she's a witch, and if she's drowned— and killed, you know—she's innocent, and not a witch, but only a poor silly old woman. But what good would it do her then, you know, when she was drowned?
>
> (bk. 1, chap. 3)

Her question is all the more poignant in light of the answer framed by the child herself: "Only, I suppose, she'd go to heaven, and God would make it up to her." As an adult, Maggie is denied even that consolation. Her fate must be idealized in order to become bearable for her creator. For only a godlike novelist can "make it up" to choiceless victims in a Godless world.

"Choose!," thunders the six-foot Tom on finding Maggie with Philip. Yet when, pages later, she does make her single choice and dutifully returns to Tom and to St. Ogg's, she does regret it. Though innocent, she must drown. As Professor Haight points out in his preface to the novel, George Eliot's contemporaries thought Maggie's escape with Stephen was terribly "wicked"; John Ruskin (whose own sexual life was hardly exemplary) accused Maggie and Stephen of "forgetting themselves in a boat"; even the more lenient Bulwer-Lytton felt that the very "indulgence" of her temptation had violated Maggie's large Ideality. The modern reader can hardly help being amused by such reactions. Sensing Maggie's kinship to Lawrence's heroines, he might easily overreact in the opposite direction and wish that Maggie had indeed "forgotten herself" with some handsome gamekeeper instead of panting like a "wounded war-goddess" after being kissed by the insipid Stephen (bk. 6, chap. 10). But such an enlightened view would be as far off the mark as that of Ruskin and Bulwer-Lytton. Like Philip Wakem, Stephen is merely a convenient device. Philip, whose femininity is repeatedly emphasized, acts as a spokesman for the novelist who likewise finds herself powerless to deflect Maggie from a predetermined course. Though impotent, Philip at least can chide Maggie for her nunlike mortifications ("stupefaction is not resignation"); a sufferer himself, the deformed artist foresees the far more bitter mortifications she will have to undergo. The pseudo-Byronic Mr. Guest, however, is primarily a listener, almost as passive as Coleridge's wedding guest. He escorts Maggie down to the boat, retreats, and reappears only as the escort of the saddened, but wiser Lucy who visits her dark cousin's grave. Maggie might have escaped alone on that river (as Romola will do in a very similar situation), but such an action would not have permitted the narrator to satirize the society which excuses Stephen but blames his female companion.

According to Professor Haight, one of George Eliot's earliest biographers, G. W. Cooke, claimed that it was not physical passion but a spiritual craving growing out of Maggie's yearning for a fuller life that led her to follow her abductor. There is at least a partial truth in this statement. Maggie's attraction to Stephen is definitely sexual (the description of her surrender is very similar to that of Hetty's submission to Arthur Donnithorne). If the feminine Philip proves to be an inadequate substitute for Tom, the broad-chested Stephen is quite as manly as Maggie's brother. Yet she follows him because she confuses sexual impulse with rational choice. Mistakenly, Maggie believes that Stephen can lead her into a better world. The child who was so completely hypnotized by the churning mill wheel had felt a "dim delicious awe as at the presence of an uncontrollable force" (bk. 1, chap. 4). The adult Maggie also wants to believe that "the tide was doing it all—that she might glide along with the swift, silent stream, and not struggle any more" (bk. 6, chap. 13). But the forgetfulness of this Lethe is imaginary. In her childhood, fantasies of a "little world apart from her outside everyday life" were always broken by Tom. Now, daylight reveals that Stephen is not the knight she had imagined him to be. Tennyson's Lady of Shalott dies when she drifts into contact with the stark reality of Lancelot's ordinary world; George Eliot's dreamy heroine dies soon after she discovers that Stephen belongs to the same prosaic world she had tried to flee. Pain is inescapable, Philip's words come true: "there is no such escape possible except by perverting or mutilating one's nature" (bk. 6, chap. 7). Stephen's own appeal to Natural Law is specious: "There is nothing in the past that can annul our right to each other," he professes (bk. 6, chap. 14). His statement applies only to his own past, not to Maggie's. Bitterly, she discovers that she is bound by that past, even if it has been lost by her father, altered by her brother, and made irrecóverable by her own growth to adulthood.

But if Maggie bows to the past, the past lacks the authority it had possessed in *Adam Bede*. To be sure, as Thomas Pinney contends, the novel's conclusion is intended to "affirm the supreme value of the early affection of Maggie and Tom for each other." But George Eliot's efforts to endow Maggie's past with a higher meaning led the novelist to inconsistencies not noted by Mr. Pinney. When Maggie and Tom become adolescents, George Eliot speaks of their having passed "the golden gates of their childhood" into a "thorny wilderness" (bk. 2, chap. 7). This remark, like the later suggestion that Maggie's affection for Philip is "tranquil" and "tender" only because it has its roots "deep down in her childhood," seems most artificially superimposed. For Tom and Maggie's childhood had hardly been "golden"; Maggie's affection for Philip could have been just as tranquil had she met the deformed young artist only as an adult at the Charity Bazaar. Even in the novel's concluding remarks, there is a definite tinge of self-deception. George Eliot allows brother and sister to relive the "days when they had clasped their little hands in love, and roamed the daisied fields together." Yet there were few instances when Maggie the child was allowed to hold her brother's hand. The little girl asked by Tom to choose between two halves of a muffin found then, as later, that any choice would make her unhappy. By resorting to the Wordsworthian myth of childhood, George Eliot apparently forgot that her heroine's agonies had begun as an infant. Maggie's first memory, after all, is that of the brother who ceases to torment her only upon his death.

For Dr. Johnson memory was not the joyful experience it was to be for Wordsworth. In one of his *Idlers,* he suggested quite realistically that the act of recollection must always be painful, since it forces us to remember the vanity of all our broken illusions. Thus, he suggested, men logically resist memory; for without its "afflictive" power the "mind might perform its functions without incumbrance, and the past might no longer encroach upon the present." The Victorians also longed for "an art of forgetfulness." Though they made a habit of repudiating the forgetfulness of lotos-eating, they, like the Doctor, fully recognized the painfulness of viewing the gaps between past and present. But the Victorian artist also derived a bittersweet satisfaction in conjuring up the lost simplicities of times past. The days when Maggie and Tom had roamed the daisied fields together may have been fictitious, as is the more openly metaphoric picture of another pair of infants toddling towards Avila in the prelude to *Middlemarch*; but it was necessary to invent that nonexistent past, to take refuge—ever so briefly—in its untroubled ways. (Had George Eliot ever written a novel about St. Theresa herself, the author would, most likely, have scaled the Spanish-woman's present against still another simpler, more innocent past.)

The fiction of childhood tranquility could at least lend meaning to Maggie's death and allow George Eliot to stir those "springs of goodness" which she had tried to touch in the death of Amelia Barton. But while she is alive, as child or adult, the complex Maggie cannot link herself to any past. Dinah could adapt the living words of John Wesley to her present; but the "Voice from the Past" which Maggie unearths in the writings of Thomas a Kempis does not speak to her own times. The author of *The Imitation of Christ* cannot really quench modern man's thirst: "She had not perceived—how could she until she had lived longer?—the inmost truth of the old monk's outpourings, that renunciation remains sorrow, though a sorrow borne willingly" (bk. 4, chap. 3). Like Savonarola in *Romola,* this monk can at best offer a concealed kernel of truth; it is Maggie's own experience, like Romola's, which must be her teacher, even if that experience leads her to death.

Maggie must eventually bear her own crown of thorns in order to imitate Christ. But, like Hetty Sorrel, she will bear her sorrow unwillingly. Her fate seems as unjust, though for very different reasons. Hetty, like Arthur, had denied the past; Maggie, on honoring the ties of the past, finds it anachronistic, bypassed by the changes inherent in all growth, evolution, and "historical advancement." The guilty Hetty did not deserve her fate because of her ignorance; the intelligent Maggie does not deserve it because of her innocence. Maggie defends Philip by saying, "He couldn't choose his father" (bk. 2, chap. 5). Neither could she. She is born and dies as the victim of chance. Despite the adequacy of the flood as a deus ex machina, despite the careful foreshadowings of the flood from the very beginning of the novel, the device, like the appearance of Stephen Guest, seems extraneous and accidental. Professor Haight detects what may well be a consciously implanted parallel to *King Lear:* "Maggie's prayer, 'O God, if my life is to be long,' is answered by the waters rising about her with something of that ironic effect of the storm that follows Lear's appeal to the gods." Yet Lear, it must be remembered, is not killed by the storm, whereas Maggie is sacrificed to the river.

In a tragedy like *King Lear*, the forces of circumstance are as prominent as in a "realistic" novel like *The Mill on the Floss*. The unexpected reversal of the French army, Edmund's deception, the protracted distraction of Albany and Edgar at the very moment that Cordelia is hanged contribute to the final tragedy. But it is Lear's initial act of willfulness, committed at the height of his powers, which has precipitated the ensuing concatenation of events. Maggie's one act of willfulness, itself blamed on the hypnotic influence of her seducer and on her Tulliver blood, is unrelated to the cataclysmic circumstances of her death. Had Lear not banished Cordelia, the carnage of his house would have been avoided; but had Maggie not fled with Stephen, she could still have drowned like the "helpless cattle" washed away by the Floss. Notwithstanding George Eliot's identification of the overflowing river with those deterministic "laws" within and without the girl's psyche, the drowning is not tragic. For all her queenly attributes, despite the carefully implanted parallels to figures like the drowning Ophelia, despite Maggie's own firsthand knowledge about "Shakespeare and everything," she remains a figure of pathos, the prey of circumstances that are capricious and accidental. There is no causal connection between her flight and the destiny assigned to her.

Indeed, had the flood occurred at the time of Maggie's and Stephen's escape, had it then prompted her belated return to the mill and led to her reunion in death with Tom, a logical connection between her willfulness and her denial of "irreversible laws" might have been established. But George Eliot wanted Maggie to drag her bloodied feet along the streets of St. Ogg's before her final canonization. The break, though it allowed the author to pour her sarcasm on the "world's wife," unfortunately robbed Maggie's death of the desired elevation by making her all the more a victim of chance like Latimer. Tom's military drillmaster complains that General Wolfe did not die heroically enough: "He did nothing but die of his wound: that's a poor haction, I consider. Any other man 'ud have died o' the wounds I've had" (bk. 2, chap. 4). The George Eliot who wept while writing about Maggie's death clearly did not consider her heroine's martyrdom to be a "poor haction." She wanted Maggie's final sojourn in St. Ogg's to be a true "Imitation of Christ." Even as a passive victim, Maggie Tulliver is infinitely more attractive than Walter Pater's indolent Marius, another unwilling imitator of Christ.

Nonetheless, there is a similarity between Pater's lifeless pagan-turned-Christian and the intensely alive daughter of a "pagan" miller. Both of these figures are the victims of chance and change; both die of the wounds which their creators resisted and survived.

The Power of Hunger:
Demonism and Maggie Tulliver

Nina Auerbach

> *Hunger was more powerful than sorrow.*
> DANTE, *Inferno*

We do not expect to meet vampires and demons on the flat plains of George Eliot's St. Ogg's, or to find witches spying on the regular rotations of the mill on the Floss. George Eliot's insistence on a moral apprehension of the real seems to banish all such strange shapes from her landscape.

But the stolid world of *The Mill on the Floss* is more receptive to the uncanny than its surface appears to be. The novel is often condemned for a loss of moral balance arising from George Eliot's overidentification with her heroine, Maggie Tulliver. It is true that Maggie's pull on the novel causes George Eliot to relinquish her sharply defined moral perspective in favor of a sense of immediate immersion in "the depths in life"—a loss of perspective that is in many ways a gain, as the author herself seems to realize, for she begins the novel by abandoning herself to her material in a refusal to be our sage. The first voice we hear is the narrator's cry for submergence in a half-drowned landscape, a defiance of the perspective of the normal: "I am in love with moistness, and envy the white ducks that are dipping their heads far into the water here among the withes, unmindful of the awkward appearance they make in the drier world above."

From *Nineteenth-Century Fiction* 30, no. 2 (September 1975). © 1975 by the Regents of the University of California.

In chapter 4, Maggie mimics the ducks' defiance of dryness and perspective by suddenly plunging her head into a basin of water, "in the vindictive determination that there should be no more chance of curls that day." The repetition of this gesture suggests an important area of experience in the novel, one that the narrator leans toward herself: plunging one's head underwater entails the exchange of a clear vision for a swimming vision, a submergence in experience at the cost of objectivity and judgment. Maggie Tulliver lives in such a swimming perspective, and *The Mill on the Floss* is her story.

Though many critics find loss of perspective to be the besetting artistic sin of *The Mill on the Floss,* the experience of perspectivelessness is in part what the novel is about. In one of its many nostalgic evocations, it defines childhood vision as "the strangely perspectiveless conception of life that gave the bitterness its intensity," admonishing us that if we could recapture this intense vision, "we should not pooh-pooh the griefs of our children." But it is part of Maggie's nature that, like Peter Pan, she never grows away from her capacity to plunge into the moment, to submerge herself exclusively in what is near. In her first intense awareness of Stephen Guest, she is "absorbed in the direct, immediate experience, without any energy left for taking account of it and reasoning about it." When she drifts down the river with him, her sensations are described as unique in their passionately immediate perspective, which gives to objects usually seen at a distance the fractured intensity of an impressionist painting: "Such things, uttered in low broken tones by the one voice that has first stirred the fibre of young passion, have only a feeble effect—on experienced minds *at a distance* from them. To poor Maggie *they were very near*: . . . and the vision for the time excluded all realities— all except the returning sun-gleams which broke out on the waters as the evening approached, and mingled with the visionary sunlight of promised happiness—all except the hand that pressed hers, and the voice that spoke to her, and the eyes that looked at her with grave, unspeakable love" (my italics). Here as so often in Maggie's life, reality is what the senses swallow undigested.

Maggie's—and George Eliot's—capacity to dissolve experience into its constituent vivid moments and sensations looks forward to Pater as much as her fostering of memory looks forward to Proust. In its emotional vividness, Maggie's renunciation seems as gratifying as her abandonment to passion, for in it she achieves not the "stupefaction" Philip envisions, but a state George Eliot defines more equivocally as "that mysterious wondrous happiness that is one with pain." What post-

Freudian critics might be tempted to dismiss as Maggie's "masochism," a neurosis that should be beneath George Eliot's noble gaze, becomes for George Eliot herself part of the virtuosity in suffering that makes a heroine: "But if Maggie had been that [wealthy and contented] young lady, you would probably have known nothing about her: her life would have had so few vicissitudes that it could hardly have been written; for the happiest women, like the happiest nations, have no history." In such passages as this, George Eliot seems to be abandoning moral placement entirely and applying a Paterian criterion of intensity to Maggie's history: the well-lived life is the vividly felt life that feeds into art. Seen in this light, the flood that justifies Maggie's life and destroys it is her only adequate consummation, because only through an upheaval of this magnitude can she attain, not merely her brother's love, but the intensity she craves from existence and cannot find there.

The fervor with which Maggie sees and is seen is thrown into relief by the emotional deadness of the medium she lives in. It is true that as a moral commentator, George Eliot gave scrupulous due to the tenacity and respectability of Tom and the Dodsons, as she herself asserted in response to Eneas Sweetland Dallas's review of the novel: "I have certainly fulfilled my intention very badly if I have made the Dodson honesty appear 'mean and uninteresting,' or made the payment of one's debts appear a contemptible virtue in comparison with any sort of 'Bohemian' qualities. So far as my own feelings and intentions are concerned, no one class of persons or form of character is held up to reprobation or to exclusive admiration. Tom is painted with as much love and pity as Maggie, and I am so far from hating the Dodsons myself, that I am rather aghast to find them ticketed with such very ugly adjectives." But no matter how tolerant and broad-minded a moralist George Eliot may be, she is disingenuous here about herself as an artist. Tom's self-denying struggle to pay his father's debts and restore the mill to the family is simply subordinated to the high drama of Maggie's love affairs with Philip and Stephen. Though we are told about his honor and ability, we are rarely allowed to see Tom at his disciplined, determined best, but only as Maggie's vindictive prosecuting angel. As for the Dodsons, occasional pious commentary about their honest virtues does not obscure the narrator's glee at the overwhelming ridiculousness of Aunt Pullet and Aunt Glegg and their muttering husbands. Nor does it counterbalance such authorial outbursts as: "A vigorous superstition, that lashes its gods or lashes its own back, seems to be more congruous with the mystery of the human lot, than the mental condition of these emmet-like Dodsons and Tullivers." This sudden endorsement of sheer intensity seems to overwhelm the novel's carefully constructed, moral antitheses.

The narrator's outburst in favor of a "vigorous," even a violent, superstition is at one with her impulse to follow the ducks and Maggie in plunging her head under water in revolt against a drier world's perspective. This tendency in *The Mill on the Floss* to oppose provincial respectability with an ambiguous emotional explosiveness that culminates in pain allies the novel with a Victorian subgenre of dubious respectability: the novel of sensation and, more particularly, the Gothic romance.

Of course, Gothic romance is in many ways alien to the George Eliot that most of us know. Her rootedness in the near mitigates against it, for Gothicism is a call of the wild, the remote in time and space. As Jane Austen's Catherine Morland puts it after Henry Tilney has led her into the sunlight of British common sense: "Among the Alps and the Pyrenees, perhaps, there were no mixed characters. There, such as were not as spotless as an angel, might have the dispositions of a fiend. But in England it was not so; among the English, she believed, in their hearts and habits, there was a general though unequal mixture of good and bad." To be Gothic is to be unadulterated and therefore un-English; and George Eliot's native tolerance seems to eschew the violent moral extremes of foreign landscapes.

Gothicism, too, is a summons from a remoter past than George Eliot wants to know; *Romola,* her one excursion into the Italian Renaissance, endows even the wild-eyed Savonarola with the secular bias and ideological complexity of an enlightened Victorian sage. Ann Radcliffe's Emily St. Aubert, on the other hand, must journey from the sunlight of home and the enlightenment of the Renaissance to a medieval Catholic setting before she can palpitate to the terrors of obscurity and night. Coleridge's ancient mariner sails from the Christian Middle Ages into a pagan and primitive seascape. Bram Stoker's Jonathan Harker and Joseph Conrad's Marlow also journey from secular contemporaneity into a haunted past, the realm of "a vigorous superstition, that lashes its gods . . . [and] lashes its own back": the world that George Eliot invokes but does not inhabit in *The Mill on the Floss.* Even Victor Frankenstein, whose researches suggest the Promethean aspirations of the "modern" scientist, travels into the past in the course of his narrative, going from the relatively stable community of an English ship to increasingly wild Alpine landscapes until he touches the primitive solitudes of Coleridge's "land of mist and snow"; moreover, his research is inspired in the first place by the medieval pseudoscience of alchemy. All Gothic journeys seem to take place in time machines.

St. Ogg's, too, "carries the traces of its long growth and history like a millennial tree," and "the Catholics," those traditional conduits of Gothic terror, are a vague threat in the novel due to the rumblings of Catholic Emancipation. But St. Ogg's is prosaically immune to its haunted past: "The mind of St Ogg's did not look extensively before or after. . . . the present time was like the level plain where men lose their belief in volcanoes and earthquakes, thinking to-morrow will be as yesterday, and the giant forces that used to shake the earth are for ever laid to sleep." The sensibly level vision of St. Ogg's is as perspectiveless as Maggie's intensely momentary one, denying the wide swings through time and space that constitute the rhythms of Gothic fiction.

George Eliot's sympathetic naturalism and her tendency to make the boundaries of the community the boundaries of reality are in some ways like the vision of St. Ogg's. Her humanistic bias is suspicious of solitary aberration, emphasizing always the "threads of connection" rather than the potentially grotesque disjunctions between people. In a famous passage from *Romola*, which is often taken as George Eliot's central statement of belief, Romola banishes the shadows of the self:

> What reasonable warrant could she have had for believing in . . . [Dino's mystical and solitary] vision and acting on it? None. True as the voice of foreboding had proved, Romola saw with unshaken conviction that to have renounced Tito in obedience to a warning like that, would have been meagre-hearted folly. Her trust had been delusive, but she would have chosen over again to have acted on it rather than be a creature led by phantoms and disjointed whispers in a world where there was the large music of reasonable speech, and the warm grasp of living hands.

Yet even within *Romola*, this declaration is ambivalent, for the solitary and irrational whisper of foreboding has proved true; and throughout the novels, George Eliot's characters turn with longing to the "disjointed whispers" of uncertain origin that come only in solitude. At the end of her career, the visionary Mordecai in *Daniel Deronda* is apotheosized as an inspired descendant of the Hebrew prophets. George Eliot's reason and trust did indeed shun solitary Gothic shadows, but her imagination did not: just before beginning *The Mill on the Floss,* she turned from the rather overinsistent naturalism of *Scenes of Clerical Life* and *Adam Bede* to write: "The Lifted Veil," a short story in which Gothic fantasies run wild. Latimer, the story's misanthropic, clairvoyant hero, comes together rather uneasily with the story's *Frankenstein*-like Alpine setting at the beginning and its reanimated corpse at the end, and George Eliot was probably right to deny her authorship of the story until 1877; but it gives us a telling glimpse of the shadows that were moving through her mind when she envisioned the dark and dreaming figure of Maggie Tulliver, standing rapt on a bridge under "the deepening grey of the sky," "like a wild thing" refusing to take her place around the family fire.

The intonations of Gothicism that run through the language of *The Mill on the Floss* converge in the "loving, large-souled" figure of Maggie, who broods over its landscape. The turbulent hair that is her bane as a child is an emblem of destructive powers she is only half aware of and unable to control; its roots reach back to the serpent tresses of the Greek Medusa, peer through the "wanton ringlets" of Milton's Eve, and stretch down from mythology into Gothicism when the female narrator of a late Victorian vampire story—Eric, Count Stenbock's "The True Story of a Vampire" (1894)—describes her "long tangled hair [which] was always all over the place, and never would be combed straight." The traditionally demonic connotations of unruly hair are reinforced by Maggie's life. The intensity with which she flings herself at the moment contains a certain murderousness, even when she is nursing a doll "towards which she [has] an occasional fit of fondness in Tom's absence, neglecting its toilette, but lavishing so many warm kisses on it that the waxen cheeks [have] a wasted unhealthy appearance." From the beginning, Maggie's kisses tend to take life rather than bestow it.

In her worm-eaten attic, she keeps another doll as a fetish, whose head she mauls and pounds into unrecognizability during outbursts of sheer violence which do not take the shape of love. Pounding her fetish, Maggie embodies "the vigorous superstition, that lashes its gods or lashes its own back" for which the narrator will pine in the desert of Dodson modernity. She turns from these two "love-dismembered" dolls to Tom, on whose neck she hangs "in rather a strangling fashion" throughout the novel, though adulthood brings her greater awareness of the draining tendency in her love: "I think I am quite wicked with roses—I like to gather them and smell them till they have no scent left." Maggie's rapacity has something in common with that of Tennyson's Ulysses, who sails away from commonality proclaiming "I will drink life to the lees"; and something else in common with that of Sheridan Le Fanu's Carmilla, a demure vampire who literally does so.

Maggie's recurrent pattern of action is to enter worlds and explode them. Her destructive aura takes shape in the associations of demonism, witchery, and vampirism that surround her, which will be examined more closely below, and which, despite the narrator's insistence on the prosaic narrowness of Lincolnshire village life, are in part an outgrowth of the environment defined by the "emmet-like Dodsons and Tullivers."

"Emmet-like" is actually an unfair dismissal of the intricacies of Dodson and Tulliver perceptions. Part, at least, of the elaborate Dodson metaphysic can be summed up in a single penetrating sentence: "it was necessary to be baptised, else one could not be buried in the churchyard." Given their tendency to embalm life's great crises in layers of ritual, it does not seem unfair to the spirit of the Dodsons to translate this sentence as, "it was necessary to be born, else one could not die." Life for the Dodsons is a tedious rehearsal for the triumphant performance of death. Aunt Glegg secretes her best hairpieces and linen, Aunt Pullet her treasured medicine bottles, Mrs. Tulliver (before the bankruptcy) her best china, so that they will be intact and pristine when that great day arrives. The aunts admire pink-and-white little Lucy, primarily because she is able to simulate the deathlike immobility of an icon: "And there's Lucy Deane's such a good child—you may set her on a stool, and there she'll sit for an hour together, and never offer to get off." It is one of the novel's muted ironies that only Aunt Deane, the most shadowy because the least Dodsonian of the sisters, achieves death in the course of the narrative. The other aunts are forced to survive beyond the end, presumably still quoting their wills and rehearsing their funerals. In a moment of uncharacteristic self-transcendence, Aunt Glegg places her husband's death before her own in this wistful reverie about the consummation of her widowhood:

> It would be affecting to think of him, poor man, when he was gone; and even his foolish fuss about the flowers and garden-stuff, and his insistence on the subject of snails, would be touching when it was once fairly at an end. To survive Mr Glegg, and talk eulogistically of him as a man who might have his weaknesses, but who had done the right thing by her . . . all this made a flattering and conciliatory view of the future.

The bristlingly proper Aunt Glegg takes the romantic Liebestod a step beyond itself: death is not merely love's climax, but its birth. Like Poe's protagonists or the converts of vampire literature, she venerates death not as a gateway to the hereafter, but as a state complete in itself, and for her its trappings and machinery are objects of fascination and delight. We need think only of such embalmed Victorian icons as Little Nell in her tomb, Tennyson's Elaine in her coffin, Millais's lavishly drowned Ophelia, to recall the loving fascination with which high Victorian art embraces and embellishes its corpses.

This reverence for and simulation of death is a pall that winds through Maggie's childhood and survives in the strikingly unnurturing quality of her love, which eats rather than nourishes its objects. When Tom comes home from school for the first time, her suggestively sterile love token is a hutch of dead rabbits for him—a symbol that Lawrence may have borrowed for *Women in Love,* in which a paralyzed rabbit becomes a token of the deathly kinship between Gerald and Gudrun. The defaced dolls, shattered cardhouses, and spoiled hopes with which Maggie's life is littered suggest that in her own messy, overheated Tulliver fashion, she inherits the Dodson penchant for death and its trappings, carrying it from respectability down toward Gothicism. The cake she crushes and the wine she spills at Aunt Pullet's have a touch of black mass in them, for example; and her love-dismembered dolls anticipate the children from whose blood all the female vampires in *Dracula* take life instead of giving it. The unwomanly, because unnurturing, woman of whom Maggie Tulliver is a small type will come into her own in vampire literature, to be hymned most erotically in the ecstatically infertile lesbianism of *Carmilla.*

Maggie's faint taste of demonism is also shot through with Tulliver blood, in an inheritance more complex than mere impulsiveness. In fact, despite her father's proud claims for his sister, Maggie's love is sufficiently nongenerative to align her with the Dodson sisters rather than with the wearily prolific Aunt Gritty, whom we can never envision defacing a doll rather than nourishing it. Maggie is closer to her father in her capacity to destroy things with the most loving of intentions, and her demonic leanings reveal an affinity with him that is intellectual as well as temperamental:

> Mr Tulliver was, on the whole, a man of safe traditional opinions; but on one or two points he had trusted to his unassisted intellect, and had arrived at several questionable conclusions; among the rest, that rats, weevils, and lawyers were created by Old Harry. Unhappily he had no one to tell him that this was rampant Manichaeism, else he might have seen his error.

The Manichaean heresy, which defines evil as an active, autonomous, and potent force rather than as the mere absence of good, expresses perfectly a world Mr. Tulliver sees madly twisting in the grip of Old Harry and his progeny. In granting to evil its own independent and powerful existence, Manichaeism is the necessary premise of Gothic sensationalism, and, like the Dodson worship of death and the deathlike, it has a powerful effect on young Maggie's sense of who she is and where she will find her life.

For Maggie's philosophical isolation, the fact that she has access to no ideology other than that of her family, is stressed again and again. Nor is the narrator able to provide one, for Maggie or for us. Her assertion of Maggie's tragic ignorance of "the irreversible laws within and without her, which, governing the habits, becomes morality, and, developing the feelings of submission and dependence, becomes religion" seems, like so much Victorian affirmation, a sonorous hedge: these "laws" are a vague postulate, unrealized in the explosive course of a novel, the mystery of whose workings may after all be most appropriately productive of a primitive and pain-ridden superstition. Lacking an overall rational structure to define our experience while reading, we are thrown back with Maggie on an ethos of sensationalism, even of demonism. To unravel her world, Maggie turns naturally to books; but they cannot provide for her the key "that would link together the wonderful impressions of this mysterious life, and give her soul a sense of home in it." Instead of opening a window into spaciousness and coherence, Maggie's books become a mirror reflecting her own dark impulses. In fact, an examination of the world she sees in books provides us with a striking portrait of Maggie herself.

As a child, Maggie invokes her demonic self out of her books. On our first extended view of her, she is poring over a picture of a witch: "O, I'll tell you what that means. It's a dreadful picture, isn't it? But I can't help looking at it. That old woman in the water's a witch—they've put her in to find out whether she's a witch or no, and if she swims she's a witch, and if she's drowned—and killed, you know—she's innocent, and not a witch, but only a poor silly old woman. But what good would it do her then, you know, when she was drowned? Only, I suppose, she'd go to heaven, and God would make it up to her."

In a passage that recalls Latimer in its near clairvoyance, Maggie projects the ambiguity of her own nature and destiny. Her interpretation of the picture is a miniature reflection of the narrator's attitude toward her: a mélange of demonism, rationalism, and a wistful faith that, after all, God will apologize in the end and redeem her innocence. But Maggie's first intuition springs out in a searing declarative statement: the woman in the water's a witch. Is Maggie? Witchery is entangled in her pull toward the smoky, nocturnal underworld of the gypsies, in "the night of her massy hair" with its suggestion of a somewhat smothering sexuality, and, most interestingly, in her charged relationship both to animals and to the natural world.

Traditional accounts of witchcraft place the witch in an intense and equivocal relationship to the animal kingdom. Animal masks are worn at the witches' Sabbath, where Satan frequently presides in the costume of a bull; animals are worshipped and used as conduits for spells, the witch's nature seeming at times interchangeable with that of her familiar. But one of the commonest manifestations of witchery is the power to blight and cause disease in the animal kingdom. Here we can see the affinity between the legends of the witch and those of the vampire. The vampire too has a magical sympathetic kinship with animals, being able to assume the shape of dog and wolf as well as bat. But in some legends, animals shun him: he is a scourge of cattle and sheep, and dogs howl and even die in terror at his approach. Both witch and vampire simultaneously spring from animals and are fatal to them.

Maggie too both blights animals and becomes them. The hutch of starved rabbits is presented as the first symbol of her love for Tom, suggesting a silent murderousness of which the animals are conduit and fetish. Yet much of the animal imagery in the novel clusters around Maggie. Her affinities with animals range from simple descriptive similes— she shakes the water from her hair "like a Skye terrier escaped from his bath"—to intimations of metamorphosis that carry magical suggestions, such as this image of Philip's: "What was it, he wondered, that made Maggie's dark eyes remind him of the stories about princesses being turned into animals? . . . . . . I think it was that her eyes were full of unsatisfied intelligence, and unsatisfied, beseeching affection." Philip's vocabulary and the narrator's reassuring explication soften the power of the picture, which is sinister. Witches in folklore are more likely to turn into animals than princesses are; and as well as expressing the rootedness of the witch in her familiar, the image evokes a string of pagan goddesses with the bodies of animals and the heads of women, of whom the lamia, the vampire's pagan ancestor, is one of the darkest.

Maggie's alliance with trees also connotes witchcraft, which is traditionally linked to tree worship: the dance around the fairy tree and invocation to it are perennial features of witches' Sabbath rituals in England. The tree appears first when little Maggie is possessed by "small demons": "a small Medusa with her snakes cropped," she pushes Lucy into the mud and retreats impenitently to the roots of a tree, to glower at Tom and Lucy "with her small Medusa face." In the sequence with Philip in the Red Deeps, the association recurs, amplified and beautified: "With her dark colouring and jet crown surmounting her tall figure, she seems to have a sort of kinship with the grand Scotch firs, at which she is looking up as if she loved them well." Philip, who seems possessed by the association of Maggie with metamorphosis, insists upon this kinship, finally painting Maggie as "a tall Hamadryad, dark and strong and noble, just issued from one of the fir-trees." Philip's artist's eye continually captures Maggie in the process of equivocal transformation, which his less true language muffles by such adjectives as "noble." To one familiar with English witchcraft legends and rituals, these images of Maggie carry their own undercurrents, which hardly need Lucy's more explicit reinforcement later on: "I can't think what witchery it is in you, Maggie, that makes you look best in shabby clothes." Another of Lucy's innocent remarks, about the secret liaison with Philip, carries more complex ironies: "Ah, now I see how it is you know Shakespeare and everything, and have learned so much since you left school; which always seemed to me witchcraft before—part of your general uncanniness." Lucy's initial intuition is correct, for Maggie learned about Shakespeare in the Red Deeps, which, as Philip senses, is the proper setting for and a powerful projection of her "general uncanniness."

But in the prophetic doppelgänger that arrests the young Maggie from the pages of Defoe, the witch is not lodged in an animal or a tree; she is bobbing in water, an element that follows Maggie and shapes her life. The origin of the English ducking ritual places the witch in a typically ambiguous relationship to water. In theory, a witch will not drown because the pure baptismal element must cast out the evil thing. But there is an obverse explanation of the witch's ability to float: perhaps her magical kinship with a more darkly defined water allies her with the element and prevents it from destroying her. The witch's dual relationship to nature is evident in the ducking ritual as it is in her power over animals: do they feed on or repel each other? Is the witch a growth from or an enemy of the natural world?

The vampire's relationship to water is as ambiguous as the witch's. In many versions of the legend, he is unable to cross running water on his own power. This abrupt paralysis is a suggestive dark gloss on the figure of the Virgin of the Flood, Maggie's holy analogue in *The Mill on the Floss,* whom local legends depict wailing by the river bank to be ferried across, unable to work her magical transformation until Beorl has allowed her to enter his boat. But Maggie's "almost miraculous" flight across the river to Tom shows her powers gushing out on the water, and so, in some stories, do the vampire's. Count Dracula feasts triumphantly on the ship's crew during an ocean voyage; he is able to control storms and tides; and Mina Harker's unholy "marriage" to him is revealed under hypnosis through a shared sense of "the lapping of water . . . gurgling by." The implicit question that runs through the legends of witches and vampires also runs through Maggie's voyages in *The Mill on the Floss:* is the pure baptismal element itself a conduit blending what is unholy with what is potentially divine?

Like the crises in the lives of Romola, Gwendolen Harleth, and Daniel Deronda, the great crises in Maggie's life come when she abandons herself to the movement of the tides. We first see her staring intently over the gloomy water; before we hear her speak, her mother prophesies darkly about her proclivity for "wanderin' up an' down by the water, like a wild thing"; her father's mad fear that irrigation will drain the mill of its water deprives her of her childhood home; the flight with Stephen that uproots so many lives takes place by water; and so, of course, do Maggie's much-criticized apotheosis and death in the final flood, which raise more questions than they resolve.

These questions are the same as those raised by the childish Maggie about the witch in Defoe who is her psychic mirror: is the woman in the water a witch or not? Does she float or sink? Is water her friend or foe, condemning her to spiritual exile forever or sweeping her to final vindication and "home"? "'O God, where am I? Which is the way home?' she crie[s] out, in the dim loneliness" of a flooded world, and the book's conclusion only echoes this cry. Everything has plunged its head under water with the ducks, as the narrator had yearned to do at the beginning. The difficult ending will always be unsatisfactory for those seeking a drier world's perspective, but it is at one with the ethos of Gothic romance as Robert Kiely defines it: "We have seen over and over again that romantic novels have troubled and unsatisfactory endings. One may say that a resistance to conclusion is one of the distinguishing characteristics of [Gothic] romantic fiction." Kiely gives a darker and more detailed account of these concluding visions in his discussion of *The Monk,* which can be translated illuminatingly into the world of *The Mill on the Floss:* "Lewis's final vision is of a chaos which neither man nor art has the capacity to control or avoid. Indeed, uncontrollable energy would seem to be the only energy there is in the world of *The Monk.* The artist, like the monk who seeks liberation from lifeless conventions, is apt to find himself unexpectedly on the side of the flood" (*The Romantic Novel in England*).

Certainly, Maggie seems to be on the side of the flood, since it seeps into the house as an efficacious, though indirect, answer to her despairing prayer. Does she "cause" it, as the vampire evokes storms and controls the tides? Are the waves on which she magically rides her final destructive ally against the commonality that expels and entices her? To some extent, at least, the flood is Maggie's last and strongest familiar, and it is not described through a soothing haze of death and rebirth imagery, but as a fury that crashes through houses, destroys livestock, and drowns crops. "Nature repairs her ravages—but not all" is the narrator's final quiet statement about a phenomenon that uproots and scars more life than it restores.

But it preserves Maggie until she has obtained Tom. Floating toward him, she is envisioned ambiguously with "her wet clothes [clinging] round her, and her streaming hair . . . dashed about by the wind." Like the witch's watery cousin, the Lorelei or mermaid, she lures Tom out of the house where he has found temporary protection—for the waters have stopped rising—into the dangerous tides. The loosely sacramental language of the ending tells us that preternatural forces have been evoked and revealed without disclosing their source. Tom is possessed by the "revelation to his spirit, of the depths in life, that had lain beyond his vision," leaving him "pale with a certain awe and humiliation." At last, "a mist gather[s] over the blue-grey eyes," he falls under Maggie's spell, rows the boat into the dangerous current, clings to her, and sinks, a devotee at last.

The mist that gathers over Tom's eyes at the end concludes the pattern of imagery that centers around what I have called the "swimming vision," a vision of eyes that project upon rather than reflect the world, associated in the novel with explosions of undirected energy reminiscent of sensationalism. Like the witch that leaps at Maggie from the pages of Defoe, the shining eyes the child sees in Bunyan reflect her own in the mask of the devil: "'Here he is,' she said, running back to Mr Riley, 'and Tom coloured him for me with his paints when he was at home last holidays—the body all black, you know, and the eyes red, like fire, because he's all fire inside, and it shines out at his eyes.'"

Throughout the novel, Maggie's potent power shines out at her eyes as the devil's does. Shortly after the above speech, we learn that the powdery white of the mill makes "her dark eyes flash out with new fire."

When "small demons" impel her to push Lucy into the mud, the Medusa-like power of her eyes is referred to twice and is demonstrated later in her bewitching effect on Philip and Stephen. Her eyes evoke Philip's vision of her as a woman metamorphosed into an animal, with its suggestions of witch, vampire, and lamia; and Stephen, after remarking prophetically "an alarming amount of devil there," falls under Maggie's spell and thirsts obsessively for her *look*. Burning or swimming, Maggie's eyes invoke or transmit more than they see, suggesting an infernal dimension to "the depths in life," that new realm which the intensity of her gaze reveals to Tom in the boat.

If Maggie uses books primarily to invoke mirror images of her own demonic tendencies, the reflections they show her may not always be malign. Bob Jakin's present of Thomas à Kempis's *Imitation of Christ* reveals to her a doctrine of renunciation and self-suppression which some critics, at least, interpret as Maggie's true path to whatever salvation the novel has to offer. At the very least, Thomas à Kempis presents Maggie with a new, celestial image of herself which prompts her to reject the books Philip offers to entice her out of isolation: Madame de Staël and Walter Scott, with their familiar, banished reflections of the "dark, unhappy ones."

But whatever Thomas à Kempis's doctrine may be in itself, it becomes in Maggie's hands another "fetish" that explodes communities and blights lives. The "law of consequences," that ethical variant of utilitarianism which operated so stringently against Arthur and Hetty in *Adam Bede,* judges actions according to their detonations on others, not the high-minded hopes that accompany them; and by its criteria at least, Maggie's applications of Kempis's strictures are disastrous. In her first liaison with Philip, renunciation erupts into hunger for love and talk and books, and clouds over Tom's triumphant restoration of the family honor—an effect which is dwelt on with greater immediacy than the checkered fulfillment of her meetings with Philip in the Red Deeps. When she falls in love with Stephen's strong arm, she renounces renunciation and momentarily abandons herself to the tides of her feeling for him; but when morning comes, the "law" she had found in Thomas à Kempis returns, somewhat transmuted in form, but even more disastrous in effect.

Maggie's second dedication to renunciation takes the form not of mystical quietism, but of a humanistic reverence for ties sanctioned by the past and kept alive by memory: "If the past is not to bind us, where can duty lie? We should have no law but the inclination of the moment."

Through this new application of Kempis, Maggie attempts to free herself from the momentariness bordering on sensationalism that has possessed her throughout her life. The "memory" she invokes is actually a myth-making faculty that makes of the past a sanctuary against the present rather than its seeding ground; and the narrator has reminded us earlier that such memories sculpted into myths can be a saving anchor against the chaos of space: "But heaven knows where that striving might lead us, if our affections had not a trick of twining round those old inferior things—if the loves and sanctities of our life had no deep immovable roots in memory."

But while adherence to memory can be a ballast, the retreat from Stephen which it results in can at that point produce only chaos. The ties to Philip and Lucy to which Maggie declares allegiance have already been snapped by her flight; Tom, the protective deity of her earliest memory, must repudiate her; memory casts her out into a present which denies her as well, containing only a shamed family, an irate community, and a devastated lover. The novel's heavy iron against "the world's wife" does not mean the wife is wrong in seeing that Maggie's wild swerve toward renunciation and her solitary return after the fact are the most destructive choices she can make. Marriage to Stephen would have hurt fewer people than a renunciation whose consequences fling Maggie and all the characters attached to her into a morass where, as the well-meaning Dr. Kenn perceives, each immediate step is "clogged with evil." In terms of its effect on other lives, even a potentially celestial book like Thomas à Kempis's can be a source of evil in Maggie's hands because, once it finds its way into her life, it does evil things.

Though in several forms the world inside books is a demonic mirror for Maggie, turning away from it to the world outside seems demonic as well. If one motif shows her avidly devouring books, another shows her obliterating them in dreams or flinging them aside. When we first meet her, she is "dreaming over her book" instead of reading it, and upon hearing Tom's name, she jumps "up from her stool, forgetting all about her heavy book, which [falls] with a bang within the fender." This sound reverberates through her first visit to Tom at school, when her abandon at seeing him again sends a fat dictionary crashing to the floor. Later on, caught in her family's dreary poverty, she dreams intermittently of using her learning to invade the world of men and so escape from home; but "somehow, when she sat at the window with her book, her eyes *would* fix themselves blankly on the out-door sunshine; then they would fill with tears, and sometimes, if her mother was not in the room, the studies would all end in sobbing." The swimming vision which is her motif in the novel leads her eyes from book to window, and thence to "fits even of anger and hatred" which "flow out over her affections and conscience like a lava stream, and frighten her with a sense that it [is] not difficult for her to become a demon." The path outward from book to nature makes of the window a demonic mirror as well, and at Lucy's house later on, her eyes move from book to window for the last time: "Lucy hurried out of the room, but Maggie did not take the opportunity of opening her book: she let it fall on her knees, while her eyes wandered to the window." Soon afterward, Maggie and Stephen will pass through this same window toward the river, in a voyage whose destructive effects we have already looked at. Both the world in books and the world beyond them are for Maggie reflections of "the depths in life" whose emissary she is forced to be in "the drier world above."

For whether they are devouring books or thirsting toward the world beyond the window, Maggie's eyes have the demonic power of transfixing and transforming what they illuminate into their own images. The power of transformation has always been central in witchcraft legends; the witch's ability to impress herself on others by fixing on them the evil eye or making of them a waxen effigy strikes at the heart of our fear that we will disappear into the image of ourselves that others see. In the two most famous nineteenth-century novels of terror, *Frankenstein* and *Dracula,* the demon's power of transformation takes on sweeping racial overtones: both the monster and Dracula threaten the human species with extinction by their hunger to propagate their own corpselike kind. If, as was said above, such female demons as Carmilla absorb some of their power from their perverse infertility, a demon with reproductive organs is more demonic still. In such a vision, evolutionary fears join with the fertility of death and the weariness of rebirth in a concluding cycle of life evolving forever into death, death into life again. The prolific destructiveness of Maggie Tulliver, the mode in which she spills into her environment by breaking and overturning things, has some of this aura. But the blight she is able to spread is crystalized in the figure of the thoroughly demonic Bertha in "The Lifted Veil," as she sits eyeing a corpse: "but I asked myself how that face of hers could ever have seemed to me the face of a woman born of woman, with memories of childhood, capable of pain, needing to be fondled? The features at that moment seemed so preternaturally sharp, the eyes were so hard and eager—she looked like a cruel immortal, finding her spiritual feast in the agonies of a dying race."

In the ensuing action of the story, the corpse Bertha eyes hungrily is actually restored to "life." Though in terms of the plot's rather awkward and incoherent machinery the reanimated corpse is Bertha's Nemesis, the conjunction between female demon with feasting eyes and the renewal of life in death is suggestive, if not causal. It reminds us that because of her fertility, the female monster in *Frankenstein* is more deadly than the male, and must be ripped savagely apart before she has been born. Apparently the nineteenth-century fear that evolution will lead to an Armageddon of demons subsuming life into death eternally is still with us, on the evidence of two contemporary American Gothic novels, Ira Levin's *Rosemary's Baby* and Thomas Tyron's *Harvest Home*. Both are pristine antifertility myths, in which the women's hunger to reproduce threatens all the norms we are supposed to cherish. Once she has been supernaturally infected, the "natural" woman casts the most dangerous shadow of all, for she is able to breed within her the germ of a new death.

George Eliot seems aware of this deeper note in her passage from the unnatural Bertha Latimer to Maggie Tulliver, who is unmistakably a woman as the author defines the species above: she is flooded by memories of childhood, an awareness of pain, and the need to be fondled. The intensity with which her womanliness is realized may obscure the extent to which Maggie, like Bertha, is spiritually feasting on the world she lives in. The language of hunger and thirst is used to define her as frequently as the nearly ubiquitous water imagery is, and its implications crystallize in an attempt to explain Philip's pull toward Maggie: "The temptations of beauty are much dwelt upon, but I fancy they only bear the same relation to those of ugliness, as the temptation to excess at a feast, where the delights are varied for eye and ear as well as palate, bears to the temptations that assail the desperation of hunger. Does not the Hunger Tower stand as the type of the utmost trial to what is human in us?"

The allusion is to the Hunger Tower where Ugolino is imprisoned in canto 33 of Dante's *Inferno*. The emotional complexity of *The Mill on the Floss* finds a precise illustration in Ugolino's life and his afterlife. In the *Inferno,* the scent of cannibalism hovers even over the love between parent and child, and its final implicit suggestion that the pain of the man who must eat is far more excruciating than that of the man who is eaten is an instructive gloss on the intimations of vampirism we have found in Maggie's avid love. Unlike that of the vampire, the horror of whose being lies in the fact that he is a body without a soul, Maggie's hunger is never denied its spirituality. Its essence is captured in a beautifully resonant line from Richard Wilbur's poem, "The Undead," an elegy for a creature who is abandoned "To pray on life forever and not possess it." The power of hunger is at one with the wish of a loving prayer. The final flood that sweeps over the novel and ravages its landscape is the last yearning efflorescence of a young woman who prays from her soul.

The suggestions of demonism we have found in Maggie Tulliver are by no means unique in George Eliot's female characters. We have already looked at the preternaturally evil Bertha in "The Lifted Veil," who in Latimer's first vision of her swims in the water imagery that always engulfs Maggie: "The pale-green dress, and the green leaves that seemed to form a border about her pale blond hair, made me think of a Water-Nixie,—for my mind was full of German lyrics, and this pale, fatal-eyed woman, with the green weeds, looked like a birth from some cold sedgy stream, the daughter of an aged river." Some of this "water-nixie" imagery also surrounds the more convincingly murderous Rosamond in *Middlemarch,* and it swarms over Gwendolen Harleth in *Daniel Deronda,* with her "lamia beauty," her green-and-white colors, her blond pallor, her sinister associations with drowning and the sea.

But George Eliot allows us to doubt whether the loveless Bertha, Rosamond, and Gwendolen are "woman born of woman." Bertha is "sarcastic," "without a grain of romance in her"; Rosamond is coldly ambitious, the riding accident that causes her to miscarry bringing with it faint memories of Hetty Sorrel's infanticide; and the involutions of Gwendolen's psychic frigidity and hatred of love are brilliantly traced. But in *The Mill on the Floss,* "if life had no love in it, what else was there for Maggie?" Although Maggie does say at one point, "I wish I could make myself a world outside [loving], as men do," George Eliot's sharp delineation of her fitful, solipsistic reading reveals that her efforts in this direction are not great. The demonism of Maggie Tulliver is planted in her very womanliness—as George Eliot defines it—and adds another dimension to the author's attitude toward a character whom many critics have accused her of overfondling. Her overt moral statements about Maggie are not always clear, but her feelings seem to have been: in Maggie Tulliver, she reveals a woman whose primordially feminine hunger for love is at one with her instinct to kill and to die. And she expresses her intertwined sense of Maggie, not in the explicit idiom of the "masculine intellect" critics have praised her for, but in the conventionally "feminine," subterranean language of the George Eliot that many deplore: the language of Gothic romance.

The Question of Language: Men of Maxims and *The Mill on the Floss*

Mary Jacobus

> *The first question to pose is therefore: how can women analyze their exploitation, inscribe their claims, within an order prescribed by the masculine? Is a politics of women possible there?*
>
> LUCE IRIGARAY, "Pouvoir du discours, subordination du féminin"

To rephrase the question: Can there be (a politics of) women's writing? What does it mean to say that women can analyze their exploitation only "within an order prescribed by the masculine"? And what theory of sexual difference can we turn to when we speak, as feminist critics are wont to do, of a specifically "feminine" practice in writing? Questions like these mark a current impasse in contemporary feminist criticism. Utopian attempts to define the specificity of women's writing—desired or hypothetical, but rarely empirically observed—either founder on the rock of essentialism (the text as body), gesture toward an avant-garde practice which turns out not to be specific to women, or, like Hélène Cixous in "The Laugh of the Medusa," do both. If anatomy is not destiny, still less can it be language.

A politics of women's writing, then, if it is not to fall back on a biologically based theory of sexual difference, must address itself, as Luce Irigaray has done in "Pouvoir du discours, subordination du féminin," to the position of mastery held not only by scientific discourse (Freudian theory, for instance), not only by philosophy, "the discourse of dis-

---

From *Critical Inquiry* 8, no. 2 (Winter 1981). © 1981 by the University of Chicago.

courses," but by the logic of discourse itself. Rather than attempting to identify a specific practice, in other words, such a feminist politics would attempt to relocate sexual difference at the level of the text by undoing the repression of the "feminine" in all systems of representation for which the other (woman) must be reduced to the economy of the Same (man). In Irigaray's terms, "masculine" systems of representation are those whose self-reflexiveness and specularity disappropriate women of their relation to themselves and to other women; as in Freud's theory of sexual difference (woman equals man-minus), difference is swiftly converted into hierarchy. Femininity comes to signify a role, an image, a value imposed on women by the narcissistic and fundamentally misogynistic logic of such masculine systems. The question then becomes for Irigaray not What is woman? (still less Freud's desperate What does a woman want?) but How is the feminine determined by discourse itself?—determined, that is, as lack or error or as an inverted reproduction of the masculine subject.

Invisible or repressed, the hidden place of the feminine in language is the hypothesis which sustains this model of the textual universe, like ether. We know it must be there because we know ourselves struggling for self-definition in other terms, elsewhere, elsehow. We need it, so we invent it. When such an article of faith doesn't manifest itself as a mere rehearsal of sexual stereotypes, it haunts contemporary feminist criticism in its quest for specificity—whether of language, or literary tradition, or women's culture. After all, why study women's writing at all unless it is "women's writing" in the first place? The answer, I believe, must be a political one, and one whose impulse also fuels that gesture toward an elusive "écriture féminine" or specificity. To postulate, as Irigaray does, a "work of language" which undoes the repression of the feminine constitutes in itself an attack on the dominant ideology, the very means by which we know what we know and think what we think. So too the emphasis on women's writing politicizes in a flagrant and polemical fashion the "difference" which has traditionally been elided by criticism and by the canon formations of literary history. To label a text as that of a woman, and to write about it for that reason, makes vividly legible what the critical institution has either ignored or acknowledged only under the sign of inferiority. We need the term "women's writing" if only to remind us of the social conditions under which women wrote and still write— to remind us that the conditions of their (re)production are the economic and educational disadvantages, the sexual and material organizations of society, which, rather than biology, form the crucial determinants of women's writing.

Feminist criticism, it seems to me, ultimately has to invoke as its starting-point this underlying political assumption. To base its theory on a specificity of language or literary tradition or culture is already to have moved one step on in the argument, if not already to have begged the question, since by then one is confronted by what Nancy Miller, in a recent essay on women's fiction, has called "the irreducibly complicated relationship women have historically had to the language of the dominant culture." Perhaps that is why, baffled in their attempts to specify the feminine, feminist critics have so often turned to an analysis of this relationship as it is manifested and thematized in writing by and about women. The project is, and can't escape being, an ideological one, concerned, that is, with the functioning and reproduction of sexual ideology in particular—whether in the overtly theoretical terms of a Luce Irigaray or in the fictional terms of, for instance, George Eliot. To quote Miller again, the aim would be to show that "the maxims that pass for the truth of human experience, and the encoding of that experience in literature, are organizations, when they are not fantasies, of the dominant culture."

But Irigaray's "politics of women," her feminist argument, goes beyond ideology criticism in its effort to recover "the place of the feminine" in discourse. The "work of language" which she envisages would undo representation altogether, even to the extent of refusing the linearity of reading. "*Après-coup,*" the retroactive effect of a word ending, opens up the structure of language to reveal the repression on which meaning depends; and repression is the place of the feminine. By contrast, the "style" of women—*écriture féminine*—would privilege not the look but the tactile, the simultaneous, the fluid. Yet at the same time, we discover, such a style can't be sustained as a thesis or made the object of a position; if not exactly "nothing," it is nonetheless a kind of discursive practice that can't be thought, still less written. Like her style, woman herself is alleged by Irigaray to be an unimaginable concept within the existing order. Elaborating a theory of which woman is either the subject or the object merely reinstalls the feminine within a logic which represses, censors, or misrecognizes it. Within that logic, woman can only signify an excess or a deranging power. Woman for Irigaray is always that "something else" which points to the possibility of another language, asserts that the masculine is not all, does not have a monopoly on value, or, still less, "the abusive privilege of appropriation." She tries to strike through the theoretical machinery itself, suspending its pretension to the production of a single truth, a univocal meaning. Woman would thus find herself on the side of everything in language that is multiple, duplicitous, unreliable, and resistant to the binary oppositions on which theories of sexual difference such as Freud's depend.

Irigaray's argument is seductive precisely because it puts all systems in question, leaving process and fluidity instead of fixity and form. At the same time, it necessarily concedes that women have access to language only by recourse to systems of representation which are masculine. Given the coherence of the systems at work in discourse, whether Freudian or critical, how is the work of language of which she speaks to be undertaken at all? Her answer is "mimetism," the role historically assigned to women—that of reproduction, but deliberately assumed; an acting out or role playing within the text which allows the woman writer the better to know and hence to expose what it is she mimics. Irigaray, in fact, seems to be saying that there is no "outside" of discourse, no alternative practice available to the woman writer apart from the process of undoing itself:

> To play with mimesis, is, therefore, for a woman, to attempt to recover the place of her exploitation by discourse, without letting herself be simply reduced to it. It is to resubmit herself . . . to "ideas," notably about her, elaborated in/by a masculine logic, but in order to make "visible," by an effect of playful repetition, what should have remained hidden: the recovery of a possible operation of the feminine in language. It is also to "unveil" the fact that, if women mime so well, they do not simply reabsorb themselves in this function. *They also remain elsewhere.*

Within the systems of discourse and representation which repress the feminine, woman can only resubmit herself to them; but by refusing to be reduced by them, she points to the place and manner of her exploitation. "A possible operation of the feminine in language" becomes, then, the revelation of its repression, through an effect of playful rehearsal, rather than a demonstrably feminine linguistic practice.

Irigaray's main usefulness to the feminist critic lies in this half-glimpsed possibility of undoing the ideas about women elaborated in and by masculine logic, a project at once analytic and ideological. Her attack on centrism in general, and phallocentrism in particular, allows the feminist critic to ally herself "otherwise," with the "elsewhere" to which Irigaray gestures, in a stance of dissociation and resistance which typically characterizes that of feminist criticism in its relation to the dominant culture or "order prescribed by the masculine." But like Irigaray herself in "Pouvoir du discours," feminist criticism remains imbricated within the forms of intelligibility—reading and writing, the logic of discourse— against which it pushes. What makes the difference, then? Surely, the direction from which that criticism comes—the elsewhere that it invokes, the putting in question of our social organization of gender; its wishfulness, even, in imagining alternatives. It follows that what pleases the feminist critic most (this one, at any rate) is to light on a text that seems to do her arguing, or some of it, for her—especially a text whose story is the same as hers—hence, perhaps, the drift toward narrative in recent works of feminist criticism such as Sandra Gilbert and Susan Gubar's formidable *Madwoman in the Attic.* What is usually going on in such criticism—perhaps in all feminist criticism—is a specificity of relationship that amounts to a distinctive practice. Criticism takes literature as its object, yes; but here literature in a different sense is likely to become the subject, the feminist critic, the woman writer, woman herself.

This charged and doubled relationship, an almost inescapable aspect of feminist criticism, is at once transgressive and liberating, since what it brings to light is the hidden or unspoken ideological premise of criticism itself. *Engagée* perforce, feminist criticism calls neutrality in question, like other avowedly political analyses of literature. I want now to undertake a "symptomatic" reading of a thematically relevant chapter from Eliot's *The Mill on the Floss* in the hope that this quintessentially critical activity will bring to light if not "a possible operation of the feminine in language" at least one mode of its recovery—language itself. I will return later to the final chapter of Irigaray's *Ce sexe qui n'en est pas un* in which an escape from masculine systems of representation is glimpsed through the metaphors of female desire itself.

II

Nancy Miller's "maxims that pass for the truth of human experience" allude to Eliot's remark near the end of *The Mill on the Floss* that "the man of maxims is the popular representative of the minds that are guided in their moral judgment solely by general rules." Miller's concern is the accusation of implausibility leveled at the plots of women's novels: Eliot's concern is the "special case" of Maggie Tulliver—"to lace ourselves up in formulas" is to ignore "the special circumstances that mark the individual lot." An argument for the individual makes itself felt by an argument against generalities. For Eliot herself, as for Dr. Kenn (the repository of her knowledge at this point in the novel), "the mysterious complexity of our life is not to be embraced by maxims." Though the context is the making of moral, not critical, judgments, I think that Eliot, as so often at such moments, is concerned also with both the making and the reading of fiction, with the making of another kind of special case. Though Maggie may be an "exceptional" woman, the ugly duckling of St. Ogg's, her story contravenes the norm, and in that respect it could be said to be all women's story. We recall an earlier moment, that of Tom Tulliver's harsh judgment of his sister (" 'You have not resolution to resist a thing that you know to be wrong' "), and Maggie's rebellious murmuring that her life is "a planless riddle to him" only because he's incapable of feeling the mental needs which impel her, in his eyes, to wrongdoing or absurdity. To Tom, the novel's chief upholder of general rules and patriarchal law (he makes his sister swear obedience to his prohibitions on the family Bible), the planless riddle of Maggie's life is only made sense of by a "Final Rescue" which involves her death: " 'In their death they were not divided.' " But the reunion of brother and sister in the floodwaters of the Ripple enacts both reconciliation and revenge, consummation and cataclysm; powerful authorial desires are at work. To simplify this irreducible swirl of contradictory desire in the deluge that "rescues" Maggie as well as her brother would be to salvage a maxim as "jejune" as "*Mors omnibus est communis*" (one of the tags Maggie finds when she dips into her brother's Latin Grammar) stripped of its saving Latin. We might go further and say that to substitute a generality for the riddle of Maggie's life and death, or to translate Latin maxims into English commonplaces, would constitute a misreading of the novel as inept as Tom's misconstruction of his sister, or his Latin. Maggie's incomprehensible foreignness, her drift into error or impropriety on the river with Stephen Guest, is a "lapse" understood by the latitudinarian Dr. Kenn. For us, it also involves an understanding that planlessness, riddles, and impropriety—the enigmas, accidents, and incorrectness of language itself—are at odds with the closures of plot (here, the plot of incestuous reunion) and with interpretation itself, as well as with the finality of the maxims denounced by Eliot.

For all its healing of division, *The Mill on the Floss* uncovers the divide between the language or maxims of the dominant culture and the language itself which undoes them. In life, at any rate, they remain divided—indeed, death may be the price of unity—and feminist criticism might be said to install itself in the gap. A frequent move on the part of feminist criticism is to challenge the norms and aesthetic criteria of the dominant culture (as Miller does in defending Eliot), claiming, in effect, that "incorrectness" makes visible what is specific to women's writing. The culturally imposed or assumed "lapses" of women's writing are turned against the system that brings them into being—a system women writers necessarily inhabit. What surfaces in this gesture is the all-important question of women's access to knowledge and culture and to the power that goes with them. In writing by women, the question is often explicitly thematized in terms of education. Eliot's account of Tom's schooling in "School-Time," the opening chapter of book 2, provides just such a thematic treatment—a lesson in antifeminist pedagogy which goes beyond its immediate implications for women's education to raise more far-reaching questions about the functioning of both sexual ideology and language. Take Maggie's puzzlement at one of the many maxims found in the Eton Grammar, a required text for the unfortunate Tom. As often, rules and examples prove hard to tell apart:

> The astronomer who hated women generally caused [Maggie] so much puzzling speculation that she one day asked Mr Stelling if all astronomers hated women, or whether it was only this particular astronomer. But, forestalling his answer, she said,
> "I suppose it's all astronomers: because you know, they live up in high towers, and if the women came there, they might talk and hinder them from looking at the stars."
> Mr Stelling liked her prattle immensely.

What we see here is a textbook example of the way in which individual misogyny becomes generalized—"maximized," as it were—in the form of a patriarchal put down. Maggie may have trouble construing "*ad unam mulieres,*" or "all to a woman," but in essence she has got it right. Just to prove her point, Mr. Stelling (who himself prefers the talk of women to star gazing) likes her "prattle," a term used only of the talk of women and children. Reduced to his idea of her, Maggie can only mimic man's talk.

Inappropriate as he is in other respects for Tom's future career, Mr. Stelling thus proves an excellent schoolmaster to his latent misogyny. His classroom is also an important scene of instruction for Maggie, who learns not only that all astronomers to a man hate women in general but that girls can't learn Latin; that they are quick and shallow, mere imitators ("this small apparatus of shallow quickness," Eliot playfully repeats); and that everybody hates clever women, even if they are amused by the prattle of clever little girls. It is hard not to read with one eye on her creator. Maggie, it emerges, rather fancies herself as a linguist, and Eliot too seems wishfully to imply that she has what one might call a "gift" for languages—a gift, perhaps, for ambiguity too. Women, we learn, don't just talk, they double-talk, like language itself; that's just the trouble for boys like Tom:

> "I know what Latin is very well," said Maggie, confidently. "Latin's a language. There are Latin words in the Dictionary. There's bonus, a gift."
>
> "Now, you're just wrong there, Miss Maggie!" said Tom, secretly astonished. "You think you're very wise! But 'bonus' means 'good,' as it happens—bonus, bona, bonum."
>
> "Well, that's no reason why it shouldn't mean 'gift,'" said Maggie stoutly. "It may mean several things. Almost every word does."

And if words may mean several things, general rules or maxims may prove less universal than they claim to be and lose their authority. Perhaps only "this particular astronomer" was a woman hater or hated only one woman in particular. Special cases or particular contexts—"the special circumstances that mark the individual lot"—determine or render indeterminate not only judgment but meaning too. The rules of language itself make Tom's rote learning troublesome to him. How can he hope to construe his sister when her relation to language proves so treacherous—her difference so shifting a play of possibility, like the difference within language itself, destabilizing terms such as "wrong" and "good"?

Maggie, a little parody of her author's procedures in *The Mill on the Floss,* decides "to skip the rules in the syntax—the examples became so absorbing":

> These mysterious sentences snatched from an unknown context,—like strange horns of beasts and leaves of unknown plants, brought from some far-off region, gave boundless scope to her imagination, and were all the more fascinating because they were in a peculiar tongue of their own, which she could learn to interpret. It was really very interesting—the Latin Grammar that Tom had said no girls could learn: and

she was proud because she found it interesting. The most fragmentary examples were her favourites. *Mors omnibus est communis* would have been jejune, only she liked to know the Latin; but the fortunate gentleman whom every one congratulated because he had a son "endowed with *such* a disposition" afforded her a great deal of pleasant conjecture, and she was quite lost in the "thick grove penetrable by no star," when Tom called out,

"Now, then, Maggie, give us the Grammar!"

Whereas maxims lace her up in formulas, "these mysterious sentences" give boundless scope to Maggie's imagination; for her, as for her author (who makes them foretell her story), they are whole fictional worlds, alternative realities, transformations of the familiar into the exotic and strange. In their foreignness she finds herself, until roused by Tom's peremptory call, as she is later to be recalled by his voice from the Red Deeps. Here, however, it is Maggie who teaches Tom his most important lesson, that the "dead" languages had once been living: "that there had once been people upon the earth who were so fortunate as to know Latin without learning it through the medium of the Eton Grammar." The idea—or, rather, fantasy—of a language which is innate rather than acquired, native rather than incomprehensibly foreign, is a consoling one for the unbookish miller's son; but it holds out hope for Maggie too, and presumably also for her creator. Though Latin stands in for cultural imperialism and for the outlines of a peculiarly masculine and elitist classical education from which women have traditionally been excluded, Maggie can learn to interpret it. The "peculiar tongue" had once been spoken by women, after all—and they had not needed to learn it from Mr. Stelling or the institutions he perpetuates. Who knows, she might even become an astronomer herself or, like Eliot, a writer who by her pen name had refused the institutionalization of sexual difference as cultural exclusion. Tom and Mr. Stelling tell Maggie that " 'Girls never learn such things' "; " 'They've a great deal of superficial cleverness but they couldn't go far into anything.' " But going far into things—and going far—is the author's prerogative in *The Mill on the Floss*. Though Maggie's quest for knowledge ends in death, as Virginia Woolf thought Eliot's own had ended, killing off this small apparatus of shallow quickness may have been the necessary sacrifice in order for Eliot herself to become an interpreter of the exotic possibilities contained in mysterious sentences. Maggie—unassimilable, incomprehensible, "fallen"—is her text, a "dead" language which thereby gives all the greater scope to authorial imaginings, making it possible for the writer to come into being.

III

We recognize in "School-Time" Eliot's investment—humorous, affectionate, and rather innocently self-loving—in Maggie's gifts and haphazard acquisition of knowledge. In particular, we recognize a defence of the "irregular" education which until recently had been the lot of most women, if educated at all. Earlier in the same chapter, in the context of Mr. Stelling's teaching methods (that is, his unquestioning reliance on Euclid and the Eton Grammar), Eliot refers whimsically to "Mr Broderip's amiable beaver" which "busied himself as earnestly in constructing a dam, in a room up three pairs of stairs in London, as if he had been laying his foundation in a stream or lake in Upper Canada. It was 'Binny's' function to build." Binny the beaver, a pet from the pages of W. J. Broderip's *Leaves from the Note Book of a Naturalist* (1852), constructed his dam with sweeping-brushes and warming-pans, "hand-brushes, rush-baskets, books, boots, sticks, clothes, dried turf or anything portable." A domesticated *bricoleur*, Binny made do with what he could find. A few lines later, we hear of Mr. Stelling's "educated" condescension toward "the display of various or special knowledge made by irregularly educated people." Mr. Broderip's beaver, it turns out, does double duty as an illustration of Mr. Stelling's "regular" (not to say "rote") mode of instruction—he can do no otherwise, conditioned as he is—and as a defence of Eliot's own display of irregularly acquired "various or special knowledge." Like Maggie's, this is knowledge drawn directly from books, without the aid of a patriarchal pedagogue. Mr. Stelling and the institutions he subscribes to (Aristotle, deaneries, prebends, Great Britain, and Protestantism—the Establishment, in fact) are lined up against the author-as-eager-beaver. Eliot's mischievous impugning of authority and authorities—specifically, cultural authority—becomes increasingly explicit until, a page or so later, culture itself comes under attack. Finding Tom's brain "peculiarly impervious to etymology and demonstrations," Mr. Stelling concludes that it "was peculiarly in need of being ploughed and harrowed by these patent implements: it was his favourite metaphor, that the classics and geometry constituted that culture of the mind which prepared it for the reception of any subsequent crop." As Eliot rather wittily observes, the regimen proves "as uncomfortable for Tom Tulliver as if he had been plied with cheese in order to remedy a gastric weakness which prevented him from digesting it." Nor is Eliot only, or simply, being funny. The bonus or gift of language is at work here, translating dead metaphor into organic tract.

Like Maggie herself, the metaphor here is improper, disrespectful of authorities, and, as Tom later complains of his sister, not to be relied on. Developing the implications of changing her metaphor from agriculture to digestion, Eliot drastically undermines the realist illusion of her fictional world, revealing it to be no more than a blank page inscribed with a succession of arbitrary metaphoric substitutions:

> It is astonishing what a different result one gets by changing the metaphor! Once call the brain an intellectual stomach, and one's ingenious conception of the classics and geometry as ploughs and harrows seems to settle nothing. But then, it is open to some one else to follow great authorities and call the mind a sheet of white paper or a mirror, in which case one's knowledge of the digestive process becomes quite irrelevant. It was doubtless an ingenious idea to call the camel the ship of the desert, but it would hardly lead one far in training that useful beast. O Aristotle! if you had had the advantage of being "the freshest modern" instead of the greatest ancient, would you not have mingled your praise of metaphorical speech as a sign of high intelligence, with a lamentation that intelligence so rarely shows itself in speech without metaphor,—that we can so seldom declare what a thing is, except by saying it is something else?

In the *Poetics* Aristotle says: "It is a great thing to make use of . . . double words and rare words . . . but by far the greatest thing is the use of metaphor. That alone cannot be learned; it is the token of genius. *For the right use of metaphor means an eye for resemblances.*" Of course there's authorial self-congratulation lurking in this passage, as there is in Eliot's affectionate parade of Maggie's gifts. But an eye for resemblances (between Binny and Mr. Stelling, for instance, or brain and stomach) is also here a satiric eye. Culture as (in)digestion makes Euclid and the Eton Grammar hard to swallow; Aristotle loses his authority to the author herself. On one level, this is science calling culture in question, making empiricism the order of the day. But there's something unsettling to the mind, or, rather, stomach, in this dizzy progression from culture, digestive tract, and *tabula rasa* to ship of the desert (which sounds like a textbook example of metaphor). The blank page may take what imprint the author chooses to give it. But the price one pays for such freedom is the recognition that language, thus viewed, is endlessly duplicitous rather than single-minded (as Tom would have it be); that metaphor is a kind of impropriety or oxymoronic otherness; and that "we can so seldom declare what a thing is, except by saying it is something else."

Error, then, must creep in where there's a story to tell, especially a woman's story. Maggie's "wrong-doing and absurdity," as the fall of women often does, not only puts her on the side of error in Tom's scheme of things but gives her a history; "the happiest women," Eliot reminds us, "like the happiest nations, have no history." Impropriety and metaphor belong together on the same side as a fall from absolute truth or unitary schemes of knowledge (maxims). Knowledge in *The Mill on the Floss* is guarded by a traditional patriarchal prohibition which, by a curious slippage, makes the fruit itself as indigestible as the ban and its thick rind. The adolescent Maggie, "with her soul's hunger and her illusions of self-flattery," begins "to nibble at this thick-rinded fruit of the tree of knowledge, filling her vacant hours with Latin, geometry, and the forms of the syllogism." But the Latin, Euclid, and Logic, which Maggie imagines "would surely be a considerable step in masculine wisdom," leave her dissatisfied, like a thirsty traveler in a trackless desert. What does Eliot substitute for this mental diet? After Maggie's chance discovery of Thomas à Kempis, we're told that "The old books, Virgil, Euclid, and Aldrich—that wrinkled fruit of the tree of knowledge—had been all laid by" for a doctrine that announces: "'And if he should attain to all knowledge, he is yet far off.'" Though the fruits of patriarchal knowledge no longer seem worth the eating, can we view Thomas à Kempis as anything more than an opiate for the hunger pains of oppression? Surely not. The morality of submission and renunciation is only a sublimated version of Tom's plainspoken patriarchal prohibition, as the satanic mocker, Philip Wakem, doesn't fail to point out. Yet in the last resort, Eliot makes her heroine live and die by this inherited morality of female suffering—as if, in the economy of the text, it was necessary for Maggie to die renouncing in order for her author to release the flood of desire that is language itself. Why?

The Mill on the Floss gestures toward a largely unacted error, the elopement with Stephen Guest which would have placed Maggie finally outside the laws of St. Ogg's. Instead of this unrealized fall, we are offered a moment of attempted transcendence in the timeless death embrace which abolishes the history of division between brother and sister— "living through again in one supreme moment, the days when they had clasped their little hands in love." What is striking about the novel's ending is its banishing not simply of division but of sexual difference as the origin of that division. The fantasy is of a world where brother and sister might roam together, "indifferently," as it were, without either conflict or hierarchy. We know that their childhood was not like that at all, and we can scarcely avoid concluding that death is a high price to pay for such imaginary union. In another sense, too, the abolition of difference marks the death of desire for Maggie; "The Last Conflict" (the title of the book's closing chapter) is resolved by her final renunciation of Guest, resolved, moreover, with the help of "the little old book that she had long ago learned by heart." Through Thomas à Kempis, Eliot achieves a simultaneous management of both knowledge and desire, evoking an "invisible" or "supreme teacher" within the soul, whose voice promises "entrance into that satisfaction which [Maggie] had so long been craving in vain." Repressing the problematic issue of book learning, this "invisible teacher" is an aspect of the self which one might call the voice of conscience or, alternatively, sublimated maxims. In "the little old book," Maggie finds the authorized version of her own and Eliot's story, "written down by a hand that waited for the heart's prompting . . . the chronicle of a solitary, hidden anguish . . . a lasting record of human needs and human consolations, the voice of a brother who, ages ago, felt and suffered and renounced."

Where might we look for an alternative version or, for that matter, for another model of difference, one that did not merely substitute unity for division and did not pay the price of death or transcendence? Back to the schoolroom, where we find Tom painfully committing to memory the Eton Grammar's "Rules for the Genders of Nouns," the names of trees being feminine, while some birds, animals, and fish "*dicta epicoena* . . . are said to be epicene." In epicene language, as distinct from language imagined as either neutral or androgynous, gender is variable at will, a mere metaphor. The rules for the genders of nouns, like prescriptions about "masculine" or "feminine" species of knowledge, are seen to be entirely arbitrary. Thus the lament of David for Saul and Jonathan can be appropriated as the epitaph of brother and sister ("'In their death they were not divided'"), and "the voice of a brother who, ages ago, felt and suffered and renounced" can double as the voice of a sister-author, the passionately epicene George Eliot. One answer, then, to my earlier question (Why does Eliot sacrifice her heroine to the morality of renunciation?) is that Eliot saw in Thomas à Kempis a language of desire, but desire managed as knowledge is also managed—sublimated not as renunciation but as writing. In such epicene writing, the woman writer finds herself, or finds herself in metaphor.

IV

For Irigaray, the price paid by the woman writer for attempting to inscribe the claims of women "within an order prescribed by the masculine" may ultimately be death; the problem as she sees it is this: "[How can we] disengage ourselves, *alive,* from their concepts?" The final, lyrical chapter of *Ce sexe qui n'en est pas un,* "Quand nos lèvres se parlent," is, or tries to be, the alternative she proposes. It begins boldly: "If we continue to speak the same language to each other, we will reproduce the same story." This would be a history of disappropriation, the record of the woman writer's self-loss as, attempting to swallow or incorporate an alien language, she is swallowed up by it in turn:

> On the outside, you attempt to conform to an order which is alien to you. Exiled from yourself, you fuse with everything that you encounter. You mime whatever comes near you. You become whatever you touch. In your hunger to find yourself, you move indefinitely far from yourself, from me. Assuming one model after another, one master after another, changing your face, form, and language according to the power that dominates you. Sundered. By letting yourself be abused, you become an impassive travesty.
>
> ("When Our Lips Speak Together")

This, perhaps, is what Miller means by "a posture of imposture," "the uncomfortable posture of all women writers in our culture, within and without the text." Miming has become absorption to an alien order. One thinks of Maggie, a consumer who is in turn consumed by what she reads, an imitative "apparatus" who, like the alienated women imagined by Irigaray, can only speak their desire as "machines that are spoken, machines that speak." Speaking the same language, spoken in the language of the Same ("If we continue to speak this sameness, if we speak to each other as men have spoken for centuries . . . we will fail each other"), she can only be reproduced as the history of a fall. Eliot herself, of course, never so much as gestures toward Irigaray's jubilant utopian love language between two women—a language of desire whose object ("*l'indifferente*") is that internal (in)difference which, in another context, Barbara Johnson calls "not a difference between . . . but a difference within. Far from constituting the text's unique identity, it is that which subverts the very idea of identity." What is destroyed, conceptually, is the "unequivocal domination of one mode of signifying over another." Irigaray's experiment in "Quand nos lèvres se parlent" is of this kind, an attempt to release the subtext of female desire, thereby undoing repression and depriving metalanguage of its claim to truth. "This wearisome labor of doubling and miming" is no longer enough.

But for all Irigaray's experimentalism, the "difference" is not to be located at the level of the sentence, as Miller reminds us. Rather, what we find in "Quand nos lèvres se parlent" is writing designed to indicate the cultural determinants which bound the woman writer and, for Irigaray, deprive her of her most fundamental relationship: her relationship to herself. In fact, what seems most specifically "feminine" about Irigaray's practice is not its experimentalism as such but its dialogue of one/two, its fantasy of the two-in-one: "In *life* they are not divided," to rephrase David's lament. The lips that speak together (the lips of female lovers) are here imagined as initiating a dialogue not of conflict or reunion, like Maggie and Tom's, but of mutuality, lack of boundaries, continuity. If both Irigaray and Eliot kill off the woman engulfed by masculine logic and language, both end also—and need to end—by releasing a swirl of (im)possibility:

> These streams don't flow into one, definitive sea; these rivers have no permanent banks; this body, no fixed borders. This unceasing mobility, this life. Which they might describe as our restlessness, whims, pretenses, or lies. For all this seems so strange to those who claim "solidity" as their foundation.

Is that, finally, why Maggie must be drowned, sacrificed as a mimetic "apparatus," much as the solidity of St. Ogg's is swept away, to the flood whose murmuring waters swell the "low murmur" of Maggie's lips as they repeat the words of Thomas à Kempis? When the praying Maggie feels the flow of water at her knees, the literal seems to have merged with a figural flow; as Eliot writes, "the whole thing had been so rapid—so dreamlike—that the threads of ordinary association were broken." It is surely at this moment in the novel that we move most clearly into the unbounded realm of desire, if not of wish fulfilment. It is at this moment of inundation, in fact, that the thematics of female desire surface most clearly.

We will look in vain for a specifically feminine linguistic practice in *The Mill on the Floss;* "a possible operation of the feminine in language" is always elsewhere, not yet, not here, unless it simply reinscribes the exclusions, confines, and irregularities of Maggie's education. But what we may find in both Eliot and Irigaray is a critique which gestures beyond cultural boundaries, indicating the perimeters within which their writing is produced. For the astronomer who hates women in general, the feminist critic may wish to substitute an author who vindicates one woman in particular or, like Irigaray, inscribes the claims of all women. In part a critic of ideology, she will also want to uncover the ways in which maxims or *idées reçus* function in the service of institutionalizing and "maximizing" misogyny or simply deny difference. But in the last resort, her practice and her theory come together in Eliot's lament about metaphor—"that we can so seldom declare what a thing is, except by saying it is something else." The necessary utopianism of feminist criticism may be the attempt to declare what is by saying something else—that "something else" which presses both Irigaray and Eliot to conclude their very different works with an imaginative reaching beyond analytic and realistic modes to the metaphors of unbounded female desire in which each finds herself as a woman writing.

George Eliot: The Law and the Father

Dianne F. Sadoff

> *The struggle between Antigone and Creon represents that struggle between elemental tendencies and established laws by which the outer life of man is gradually and painfully being brought into harmony with his inward needs.*
> GEORGE ELIOT, "The Antigone and Its Moral"

In *The Mill on the Floss,* Mrs. Glegg writes her will strictly on the "fundamental fact of blood"; despite what she regards as Mr. Tulliver's disreputable behavior to her sisters, her legacies "bear a direct ratio to degrees of kinship." In *Felix Holt the Radical,* Mrs. Transome takes pride in her genealogy and analyzes the world solely in terms of "blood and family." The Transome matriarch and the women of the Dodson clan—who store and hoard their belongings so as to will them to their survivors—believe all legal matters can be resolved on the basis of kinship and genealogy: the law is based on maternity and on the structures of the family. *The Mill on the Floss* and *Felix Holt* also seem to define the law as a matter of paternal precedence. Mr. Tulliver owns Dorlcote Mill by virtue of one hundred years of family possession; Pivart, who has recently bought the farm upstream, therefore has no right to meddle with the Floss's water-flow. According to Tulliver, "water is water," and his right to the water is based on the genealogy of fathers who will the mill to sons: a son inherits land from his father, who inherited it from his father, and so he inherits the privilege and authority that go with ownership. Tulliver continually "goes to law" thinking patrimony guarantees him legal right to water, bridge crossings, and footpaths. In contrast, old Mr.

From *Monsters of Affection: Dickens, Eliot, and Brontë on Fatherhood.* © 1982 by the Johns Hopkins University Press, Baltimore/London.

Transome, the patriarchal figure of genealogy and property transmission in *Felix Holt,* appears foolish and mad. But Transome is not that patriarch. The novel seeks as it repeatedly invokes "the truth," and the narrative's "whole truth" resides in Jermyn's words to Harold Transome: *"I am your father."* When Harold discovers his illegitimacy, he assumes he has no legal right to Transome Court and feels it his duty to offer the family's property to Esther, its rightful inheritor.

These two narratives link fatherhood with legal rights, inheritance, and authority. A father determines his progenies' privileges, duties, and properties; he empowers the structures of inheritance by virtue of having engendered offspring. Eliot's legal and genealogical metaphor enables the father to determine legitimacy and to wield authority based on precedence. In his theories about paternity and symbolism, Jacques Lacan also links the father, authority, and law: the signifier of the Father is "author of the Law." Lacan drew on Freud's *Totem and Taboo,* in which the symbolic murder by the sons of the precedent and authoritative father celebrates both their rebellion against him and their internalization of his prohibition against incest. Lacan's version of law is based less equivocally on prohibition: the law is constituted by the father's "no." When Lacan's sons metaphorically murder the father, they bind themselves as subjects "for life to the Law," to certain symbolic structures, to the cultural prohibition against incest, to a positionality in the chain of signifiers that is culture and language. Lacan sees as causal, then, the relationship between the father as signifier and the acquisition by the child of cultural prohibitions and symbolism. By "signifier," I think Lacan means that the "father" exists in a chain of desire and prohibition the structure of which, like that of language, can be understood to transform and codify itself according to certain laws—a notion that grows out of Freud's increasingly structural topologies not only of the unconscious and its functions but of the Oedipus complex as well. In contrast, the symbolic Father, the Father upon whose name religion teaches us to call, "signifies this Law." Culturally authoritative and prohibitive paternity facilitates the real father's "no" and structures the symbolism to which the child must accede.

The authoritative and prohibitive father appears in Mary Ann Evans's first texts, her letters. Here she links fatherhood, authority, filial duty, and property (or domicile) just as George Eliot links them in her legal narratives. For Mary Ann Evans, these issues center on her role as her father's housekeeper. In 1837, she succeeded to the role of "mistress" of Griff. This official social and housekeeping role provided Mary Ann a sense of "usefulness" and autonomy which allowed her to welcome friends "independently" at her own home. It must also have facilitated her sense of personal authority; Dorothea Brooke, for example, who performed the same role for her bachelor uncle, "did not at all dislike her new authority, with the homage that belonged to it." In 1840, however, the possibility of her brother Isaac's marrying and so making his new wife mistress of Griff threatened Mary Ann's role as her father's housekeeper. For a period of nearly ten months, Mary Ann did not know either her future domicile or role. Would she live with her older sister at Meriden, or would her father take her with him as housekeeper to a new home? This uncertainty, she wrote her Aunt and Uncle Evans, "unhinge[d her] mind a little," although she wished to "imitate" her "father's calm endurance and humble gratitude and be quite free from anxiety respecting [her] destination."

Mary Ann happily continued her role as her father's housekeeper at Foleshill once his decision was made. Yet within another ten months, Mary Ann refused to attend church with her father. In the "Holy Wars" that followed, as Mary Ann later called them, father and daughter struggled over filial obligation and paternal authority. This act of rebellion caused Mary Ann another period of uncertainty about her future domicile and role: Robert Evans threatened to leave Foleshill for Packington Cottage, blaming Mary Ann for the expenditure of money needed by married sisters and brothers. Mary Ann visited Griff while her father again refused to decide her destiny. When she agreed once more to attend church with him, Mary Ann's father reinstated her as mistress of Foleshill, although she nevertheless reserved for herself the right not to listen to the church service. These two episodes define a father's complete authority over an unmarried daughter's destiny. He and he alone controls the domicile and role that create her sense of personal authority and daughterly duty.

Father and daughter struggle not only over authority but over symbolism and signification as well. The father's authority resides in his position of precedence and in his gender; his word, his prohibitive "no," constitutes the law to which his child must bind herself. The language of the father's authority, then, promulgates the law; his prohibitive word must be trustworthy, his promise acceptable. But although Robert Evans maintained total control over his daughter's future, he refused to speak clearly the language of paternal authority. Mary Ann noted to Cara Bray, "Unless I draw a circle round [my father] and require an answer within it, he will go on hesitating and hoping for weeks"; to Abigail Pears, "I must have a *home*, not a visiting place. I wish you would learn something from my Father, and send me word how he seems disposed." Lacan discusses this paradox of fatherhood in his essay on Judge Daniel Paul Schreber: the more completely the real father claims the function of legislator, the more opportunities he creates for himself of failing as the ideal promulgator of the law. His word, his authority, may therefore appear undeserved, inadequate, or fraudulent. This gap between the language of authority and its representative speaker in the family makes the law itself suspect. In the "Holy Wars," Robert and Mary Ann Evans played out this struggle in a symbolic arena. As Ruby V. Redinger points out, the rebellion against a Heavenly Father's authority appears to be a displaced act of rage against an earthly father's authority. Although her real father maintains authority over his daughter, that daughter refuses to allow the symbolic Heavenly Father to do the same. She declares His Word suspect, inadequate, and fraudulent; denies her obligations and duties to a symbolic Father; refuses to call on His Name or to listen to the words of veneration and worship of Him. Yet the symbolic veneration of the Father which indeed calls on His Name structures the cultural and linguistic systems in which the child must situate herself. Mary Ann's eventual compromise recalls the totem meal of Freud's murdering sons: while rebelling against a father's law on one level, she fully accepts his authority on another and so binds herself to his word for life.

Eliot's legal narratives play out this ambivalent attitude toward paternal law. While *The Mill on the Floss* and *Felix Holt* assert the father's precedence as conferring authority, they also demonstrate the cultural decline of paternity as a legal and lawful category. Paternal precedence in fact no longer determines and defines ownership, its rights and duties. Each time Tulliver "goes to law," the lawyer Wakem outsmarts him. Wakem eventually owns Dorlcote Mill, and when Tulliver goes bankrupt, Wakem controls the right to its tenancy; Tulliver then remains on the land of his grandfathers only at Wakem's pleasure. *Felix Holt's* lawyer (and father), Matthew Jermyn, manipulates the law as skillfully if more corruptly than does Wakem. He controls the Transome land and timber by illegal use of the settlement laws; his past adultery with Mrs. Transome and resulting fatherhood of Harold Transome consolidate his power. In *The Mill,* the law as metaphor demonstrates the decline of legal rights and duties based on the concept of kinship and the simultaneous rise of monetary obligation based on business dealings. After the old-fashioned father Tulliver falls off his horse and into bankruptcy, his son rises into the professional management class. In *Felix Holt,* the law as metaphor demonstrates the decline of rights, duties, and ownership based on aristocratic paternal precedence and the concomitant rise of democracy. The novel's historical setting—just after the Reform Bill of 1832—enables Eliot to link the ownership of small parcels of land not inherited from fathers with the rights and duties of suffrage and participation in the political process. Whereas Eliot's nostalgic narrator in *The Mill* bemoans the loss of kinship as the basis of law and figuratively portrays this change in his histories of Rhine versus Rhone, his history of St. Oggs juxtaposed with the personal destiny of the business-minded Mr. Glegg, the narrator of *Felix Holt* understands fully the inevitability—if not the desirability—of this change. Both *The Mill* and *Felix Holt* represent social rights and privileges as no longer residing in lawful paternal precedence and authority, in patriarchal succession—although Eliot may well wish they still did.

In virtually all her early narratives, Eliot in fact questions the authority of her fictional fathers. Their competence appears problematic because they fail in the symbolic arena of language: they misinterpret the signs and symbols around themselves. Mr. Tulliver cannot read "the maze of this puzzling world" and so can only disentangle the threads of this complex web by pulling on one thread, by grabbing single-mindedly at one clue as that which unriddles the puzzle. Tulliver's simplistic metaphors—the law as "cock-fight," for example—indicate not only his failure to interpret a complex world correctly but his failure to understand as well that it must be interpreted. Sir Christopher Cheverel, Tina's adoptive father in "Mr. Gilfil's Love-Story," misinterprets Tina's love for his son as love for the bungling Mr. Gilfil; "I thought I saw everything," he later moans, "and was stone-blind all the while." Adam Bede, whose character Eliot based on her father's, fails to interpret Hetty's blush when he and she pick currants, thinking "the signs of love for [Arthur] . . . signs of love towards himself." Like Tulliver, Adam misunderstands that "nature's language" needs interpretation. He assumes that Hetty's physical beauty is a sign of her character and that he as what the narrator calls a "great physiognomist" can read nature's writing in the "exquisite lines" of her face. Amos Barton, whom Eliot's narrator ruthlessly satirizes as the "quintessential extract of mediocrity," fails to recognize the signs of Milly's love or to interpret the stories about his supposed relationship with the Countess Czerlaski. In his professional life, Amos fails to understand that preaching must be tailored to suit his flock. He lectures poor people with exegetical "types and symbols" and refuses to bring his university-educated mind "to the pauper point of view." In contrast, the Reverend Cleves preaches sermons the "wheelwright and the blacksmith can understand" because he calls a "spade a spade" and moves freely among the people.

The fictional father's inability to interpret the world as different from or other than himself names him as Eliot's first egoist. Virtually all the fathers I have considered willfully misinterpret events because of paternal pride. Mr. Tulliver fails to realize that his pride drives him to "go to law" and so causes his eventual bankruptcy. Tulliver's obstinacy prevents him from interpreting his own behavior as self-indulgent; his debt to Mrs. Glegg, for example, need not have been paid off immediately but for his arrogance. In contrast, Sir Christopher Cheverel realizes he has "been too proud and obstinate" and should forgive his sister for marrying against his will. He reforms and takes his sister's son as his new heir. Likewise, Adam Bede eventually understands his pride and severity of character and vows never to be "hard" again. He bends his otherwise iron willfulness and recognizes he should have been generous with his now-dead father and with Hetty Sorrel. In each of these early narratives, the father's inability to interpret language and events around him as different from his wishes also creates a catastrophe that culminates in death, murder, or attempted murder. Amos Barton's ignorance inflicts death upon his long-loving wife as surely as does the Countess's selfishness; Sir Christopher's insistence that Tina marry Mr. Gilfil intensifies her passion for Wybrow and in turn helps cause her desperate theft of the dagger; Adam Bede's misreading of Hetty's love and resulting proposal of marriage drive her to murder her child as surely as does her illicit passion for Arthur Donnithorne. The fictional father's complicity in the crimes of passion makes him responsible for causal events in the "inexorable law of consequences" upon which Eliot's narratives insist so sternly.

The fictional father's misinterpretation intensifies the suffering of others and so inflicts suffering and punishment upon himself. This severe and authoritative father must learn sympathy through suffering. In *Adam Bede*, Eliot articulates this moral fully: "Whenever Adam was strongly convinced of any proposition, it took the form of a principle in his mind. . . . Perhaps here lay the secret of the hardness he had accused himself of: he had too little fellow-feeling with the weakness that errs in spite of foreseen consequences. . . . And there is but one way in which a strong determined soul can learn it—by getting his heart-strings bound round the weak and erring, so that he must share not only the outward consequence of their error, but their inward suffering." Steven Marcus defines Eliot's doctrine of sympathy as the enabling social sentiment, as the power of communication among members of a community. Sympathy thus serves to control conflict and to expunge alienation and radical negativity from a community. But it also serves to humiliate figures of authority: aristocrats, clerics, fathers. Adam Bede, as Eliot's brother Isaac recognized, is based on the author's memories of her father. In learning the lesson of sympathy through suffering, Adam learns what Robert Evans refused to contemplate. Adam binds himself to a law of a woman who preaches the authoritative doctrine of fellow-feeling; in writing *Adam Bede,* Eliot metaphorically binds her father to her own moral law of sympathy—a sympathy she was forced to learn when she lost the Holy Wars to her father. In *Adam Bede,* Adam's and Dinah's sympathy forgives a passionate woman, Hetty Sorrel, her transgressions and facilitates the mature love of Adam for Dinah. Eliot's doctrine of sympathy, moreover, accuses the fictional father of coldness. When Amos Barton leaves Shepperton after losing his curacy, he visits Milly's grave and speaks the words, "Milly, Milly, dost thou hear me? I didn't love thee enough—I wasn't tender enough for thee—but I think of it all now." Amos's misinterpretation, his refusal to see that the stories of the community demand interpretation, his arrogance, all come to this: he did not love his wife enough. And Amos's realization, the narrative implies, will increase his affection for and attention to his daughter. Eliot's morality of sympathy, then, serves her early narrative project: it humbles—dare we say humiliates?—the fictional father, demonstrates his authority inauthentic, and focuses his care on a daughter.

If Eliot declares the father arrogant and a failure in the realms of signification and authority, however, she also wishes him to be the lawgiver. Mr. Tulliver speaks to his daughter the language of love in the scene of seduction, as we have seen, but he also fails to discipline her. When he buys Maggie back from the gypsies, Mr. Tulliver refuses to punish her and demands that Mrs. Tulliver not reproach and Tom not taunt Maggie. Yet Maggie's absolute hunger for love, her rage and vengeance when she is denied it, demonstrate her concomitant need for discipline. Mr. Tulliver promulgates no law, utters no word of authority to his daughter. As a result, Tom provides Maggie the discipline and punishment her father refuses her. When she inadvertently kills his rabbits, cuts her hair, and pushes Lucy in the mud, Tom rebukes and taunts her. Yet Maggie continues to act in ways that encourage Tom's disapproval; narratively, Maggie appears to desire his rejection and punishment. Although Laura Comer Emery and David Smith describe Tom and Maggie's relationship as incestuous, Maggie's endearments to and caresses of

Tom and her desire to live always with her brother repeatedly facilitate not fulfillment of her desire but punishment for what she herself considers her naughtiness. When he grows up, Tom continues to punish Maggie for her desire: he refuses her the companionship of Philip Wakem and severely rebukes her for sexually desiring and running away with Stephen Guest—as her father failed to punish her for running away to the gypsies. Tom speaks the authoritative word of repudiation which defines Maggie's failure to bind herself to the laws of the community:

> Her brother was the human being of whom she had been most afraid, from her childhood upwards: afraid with that fear which springs in us when we love one who is inexorable, unbending, unmodifiable—with a mind that we can never mould ourselves upon, and yet that we cannot endure to alienate from us. . . . She almost desired to endure the severity of Tom's reproof, to submit in patient silence to that harsh disapproving judgment against which she had so often rebelled: it seemed no more than just to her now—who was weaker than she was? She craved that outward help to her better purpose which would come from complete, submissive confession—from being in the presence of those whose looks and words would be a reflection of her own conscience. . . . "You will find no home with me. . . . You have disgraced my father's name."

The language of desire clearly names Maggie's urge to be punished in this passage; she "craves" harsh and severe judgment, desires discipline that will teach her society's law. Tom represents her conscience and so speaks the word that banishes Maggie from her home by invoking the name of a father. Tom resembles the willful and severe Adam Bede before Adam learns not to be "hard," yet this narrative shows the daughter needing the authoritative severity the earlier one repudiated. Tom's harsh judgment of Maggie appears narratively correct (although we sympathize with Maggie's exile), and he need not learn the lesson of sympathy through suffering as Adam Bede once did.

Tom's role as lawgiver establishes him as the figurative father whom Maggie desires will punish rather than love her. The narrative in fact insists metaphorically and structurally on the brother as figurative father. When Gritty Moss compares her relationship with her brother, Mr. Tulliver, to the relationship of Maggie and Tom, Tulliver recognizes the truth of her analogy. He treats Gritty with tenderness only because he fears if he is severe with his sister, Tom will be "hard and cruel" to *his* sister, Maggie. In addition, although the narrative appears to support the Dodson clan's belief that Tom resembles them rather than the Tullivers, Tom in fact resembles his father. He proves as "contrary as his father"; his "Rhadamantine" urge to deal "justice that desires to hurt culprits as they deserve to be hurt" merely exaggerates the "love of retributive justice" that continually drives his father to the law. Tom is educated to business because Mr. Tulliver fears his son's desire to usurp the paternal property, and the narrative indeed proves this desire true. After his father's "downfall," Tom enters the peddling business, rises to join Mr. Glegg's firm, pays his father's debts, buys back the mill he now rents from Wakem, and becomes the mill's "master." He fills the place a father vacated and fills it with more authority than did the father. *The Mill on the Floss* splits the father in two: one father desires the desiring daughter, the figurative other prohibits and punishes all her desire. No narrative conclusion can reconcile the opposition inherent in this narrative structure. As Eliot must have known when she researched inundations before beginning the novel, only the flood that paradoxically fulfills and sweeps away desire can overcome this motivational split.

The father who is taught sympathy and the figurative father who punishes exist as a dichotomy in Eliot's early narratives. These irreconcilable fictional fathers and the narrative structures they inhabit find their source in the dialectic of desire and prohibition which structures the female Oedipus complex. For Lacan's version of the child binding himself to the law and to the symbolic structures of culture and language through the father's prohibitive word pertains only to sons. How does a daughter bind herself to the law? I will discuss the female castration complex and the daughter's shifting her love from mother to father [elsewhere]; here, I would like to characterize the problematic love between father and daughter. For at this difficult time, the daughter must confront her father as a figure of both desire and prohibition. To win his love, she must please him; she must express her love for him yet obey his law or risk his disapproval and punishment. Freud believes that because the daughter desires the figure of the law, she creates a weaker superego than does the son. I would say instead that she identifies with the father's authority less strongly than does the son; his role as model for conscience is tempered by her desire for him. Moreover, if she incorporates into herself even a modified version of the father's prohibition, must the daughter also deny her own desire? According to Nancy Chodorow, the daughter's desire for the father is less fundamental than the son's for the mother; a daughter's primary attachment to the preoedipal mother means a girl's desire for the father is always tempered by her first choice of love object. Given that Victorian mothers (or their female surrogates) performed early infant child care and given the power of Victorian fathers, self-sacrifice in the realm of authority and self-mutilation in the realm of desire appear probable for this historical daughter.

Because of asymmetry in the male and female Oedipus complex, the daughter also enters the realm of culture problematically. What role, for example, does the daughter play in the symbolic murder of the father by the primal sons? Must she also metaphorically murder the father who was once her rival for the mother to accede to the structures of culture or to achieve the positionality required to define herself as subject? Clearly not. Indeed, the son entering the social order learns that he must renounce his mother because she belongs to his father, who has the power to punish his desire with the loss of his masculinity: the incest taboo. But the son also learns he will grow up to have his own woman, and he may also have a daughter. The girl receives no such compensation or reward for renouncing the Oedipus complex. The daughter entering the social order learns she may possess neither mother nor father, and she will one day be possessed by someone like her father. She will be exchanged by sons as confirmation of the pact that signifies the incest taboo. The daughter therefore has little incentive to give up the "haven" of the Oedipus complex, as Freud defines it; she need not give up the father, figure of approbation and discipline. Desire and prohibition, authority and submission, law and dependency, then, structure the female Oedipus complex and make the father-daughter bond an ongoing issue for the Victorian daughter.

In her letters before and after Robert Evans's death, Eliot portrayed her relationship with her father as loving and disciplining. Despite her deprivation of loving words from her father, as I discussed [elsewhere]. Mary Ann wrote to Cara Bray while her father was dying: "The one deep strong love I have ever known has now its highest exercise and fullest reward—the worship of sorrow is *the* worship for mortals." This deep love for a father who failed to reciprocate feeling appears to have bred a concomitantly deep dependency. "What shall I be without my Father?" Mary Ann asked herself. "It will seem as if a part of my moral nature were gone. I had a horrid vision of myself last night becoming earthly sensual and devilish for want of that purifying restraining influence." Without a father's authority and prohibition, without the strictures of duty, obligation, and self-discipline imposed upon her by that father and her role as his housekeeper, Mary Ann Evans feared regressing into the evangelical Mary Ann, ruled by religious rhetoric and evading with useless confession her passions and feelings, her raw desire. When she returned from Switzerland after her father's death, Mary Ann realized, "We are apt to complain of the weight of duty, but when it is taken from us, and we are left at liberty to choose for ourselves, we find that the old life is the easier one." Having depended upon a father's authority for her own self-authority and upon a father's laconic expression of care for satisfaction of her desire, this daughter felt lost and without purpose without her father. That life with father, its deprivations and disciplines, now appeared preferable to the life in which she must define her desires apart from a father and discipline herself without his authoritative word. When with the help of George Henry Lewes, George Eliot was created, Mary Ann Evans began to work through this problematic father-daughter material about desire and authority.

Eliot's narrative dilemma in the early novels, then, comes to this: a fictional father is humbled and so binds himself to a daughter's moral law, or a daughter humbles herself in attempting to bind herself to a figurative father's and the community's law. When Amos Barton, Sir Christopher Cheverel, and Adam Bede lose their authority, they become Mr. Tulliver, the ineffective and bankrupt father. As Patty Barton emerges from anonymity, she becomes Maggie Tulliver, the daughter as subject of her story of desire and punishment. I treat Eliot's early narratives as one text to introduce two theories the remainder of this chapter will test. First, when the father loses his authority, the narrator acquires it; second, when the daughter becomes subject of the phrase and story, "a father seduces a daughter" ("a daughter seduces a father"), the narrative blames her for the structures of desire and punishes her accordingly. *Romola,* as I shall argue [elsewhere] confronts this problematic prohibition and desire and attempts to put to rest father-daughter thematics: Savonarola and the narrator of *Romola* promulgate the moral law more severely than did the "hard" fictional father, Adam Bede; the daughter must learn willingly to accept chastisement for her desiring willfulness.

Romola was written between Eliot's two narratives about the family and law, *The Mill on the Floss* and *Felix Holt.* I would like to explore some differences between them which I deferred at the beginning of this discussion of law and the father. Whereas Maggie fluctuates between demonic desire and the self-humiliating need to be punished, Esther Lyon outgrows her desire—her "vanity"—and accepts the "law, and the love that gave strength to obey the law." Desire has been transmuted into sympathy, law into order. The later narrative daughter learns the sympathy and fellow-feeling a father once learned. "Father, . . . I have not loved thee enough," she tells Rufus Lyon, her adoptive father, and her words echo Amos Barton's, "Milly, I did not love thee enough." This daughter must also willingly choose to obey the doctrine of sympathy. Esther Lyon sets this morality against patrilineal law and chooses not to inherit the land that is rightfully hers but to marry Felix. When desire becomes sympathy and the father's prohibition becomes moral law, what does Eliot portray as a daughter's destiny? Esther tells her future husband she is weak and he "must be greater and nobler" than she; Felix preaches against wealth, chooses to remain a member of the working class, and opens a night school to convert the rowdy workers to sobriety and family responsibility. Eliot's conjoining of love and law in the figure of Felix Holt appears to express standard Victorian morality both abstract and conservative. It contains the potential challenges of uppity daughters and so plays into the hands of political conservatism; it adjures members of the working and lower classes to be content with their place in society without questioning the class structure that defines them as morally inferior. Eliot has not successfully resolved her narrative dilemma or put to rest her paternal thematics. Despite her efforts in *Romola,* law and desire continue to preoccupy George Eliot's narrative project.

Eliot, Wordsworth, and the Scenes of the Sisters' Instruction

Margaret Homans

Two of Wordsworth's most important lyrics about the growth of the poet's imagination, "Tintern Abbey" and "Nutting," are also the scenes of a sister's instruction. Different as these two poems are, at the end of each the poet turns unexpectedly to his sister (named either as a sister or, in the case of "Nutting," as "dearest Maiden"), who enters the poem not in her own right but in answer to the poet's and the poem's needs. At the end of "Tintern Abbey," the poet exhorts the sister to "remember me" by living out the stages of youth to which he himself cannot return. The last three lines of "Nutting" frame the poet's painfully earned knowledge with the address, "Then, dearest Maiden," so as to turn that knowledge into instructions:

> Then, dearest Maiden, move along these shades
> In gentleness of heart; with gentle hand
> Touch—for there is a spirit in the woods.
>
> (ll. 54–56)

Both sisters exist to receive the brother's wishes, to confirm for him his hope that what he has gained in the course of the poem will find a habitation in a consciousness perhaps more enduring than his own. We do not expect to learn anything from her about how she will use the gift contained in the poet's words. Her quietude verifies the power of the poet's performative words: he speaks, and for her to hear his words is, implicitly, to enact them. To ask what this listening might mean to her

From *Bearing the Word: Language and Female Experience in Nineteenth-Century Women's Writing.* © 1986 by the University of Chicago. University of Chicago Press, 1986.

is a question that the text itself excludes; yet for George Eliot it is a real one, as it was also for the poet's sister. What is the female listener (or reader) to do with these words that are intended to help her avoid the painful experiences that have forged the poet's consciousness? What does it mean to follow instructions given, not for the sake of the student, but for the sake of the teacher? The poet implies that the sister he addresses will learn to follow his path if she follows his instructions, but how are they to be followed, and with what results? These are not Wordsworth's concerns, but they are Eliot's.

Mary Ann Evans's remarks on reading Wordsworth at the age of twenty suggest that while, like Wordsworth's ideal sister, her feelings are congruent with his, she also experiences some ambivalence about receiving the poet's instructions. "I have been so self-indulgent as to possess myself of Wordsworth at full length. . . . I never before met with so many of my own feelings, expressed just as I could like them." She does wish to be instructed: "to possess myself of" admits to a foreign excellence that must be possessed as different, not simply recognized. Yet simply to accept the poet's words would be, like the sister in the poems, to remain silent. That she describes her reading as "self-indulgent" and as a recognition of her "own feelings" suggests that, even though it is done half-jokingly, she needs to diminish Wordsworth's power of suggestion and to make it clear that any act or feeling the poet describes was hers before she learned that it might seem derivative. Moreover, the phallic formulation, "possess myself . . . at full length," suggests an aggressive role reversal that puts Wordsworth in the subordinate position. This tension between the need to respect and the need to deny a powerful influence—the feeling that what she possesses herself of, she had already possessed—is representative of the attitude toward Wordsworth expressed later on in Eliot's works.

Eliot's ambivalence toward Wordsworth's authority has been magnified for modern readers by a certain critical predisposition. Most readers who identify Wordsworthian features in Eliot have simply demonstrated affinity or resemblance without raising the question of derivation, taking Mary Ann Evans's word for it that Eliot's mind converged spontaneously with Wordsworth's on the same point. Had there been no Wordsworth, Eliot would still have discovered for herself what are commonly taken to be their shared beliefs in the value of childhood and rural life and in the necessity of constant interchange between feeling and knowledge. But while these are freely granted to be Eliot's own beliefs, criticism has nonetheless continued to comment on her Wordsworthian qualities (just as it has sought out her Feuerbachian and Comtean qualities). Perhaps this is because believing her philosophic power imitates male originals (like her pseudonym) allows readers to portion out among various male authors some of the respect Eliot commands, much as the belief that [Mary] Shelley was a passive reflection of her husband's views has, as we have seen [elsewhere], served to diffuse the impact of *Frankenstein*. It is generally assumed that Eliot's Wordsworthianism is pure, oddly, for two opposing reasons: the respect critics feel for George Eliot's originality is so great that they do not think of calling "him" derivative; but their knowledge that "he" is really only Mary Ann Evans prepares them to find a daughterly veneration that would never tamper with literary authority. Criticism's need to find Eliot derivative not only highlights her own ambivalence but also situates the question of that ambivalence in the question of gender. For critics could not possibly have been so concerned to see authority so docilely obeyed if the genders in the case were reversed.

Despite criticism's collusion with Eliot, there are a number of incongruities between Wordsworth's ideas and Eliot's texts that seem more than simply differences, scenes and passages that Eliot invites her readers to find Wordsworthian while she indicates a significant pattern of divergence from his prototypes. The brotherly instructions that Eliot is most generally concerned at once to follow and to deny are contained in Wordsworth's wish, in the verse of "Prospectus" to *The Recluse,* to see "Paradise, and groves / Elysian" be "A simple produce of the common day" (ll. 47–48, 55). But when she follows this wish literally, her "common day," the intensely social world of her novels, tests far more strenuously the adaptability of the paradisal vision than does anything Wordsworth wrote. The generic incompatibility between a poet's vision and the form of the novel may account for some of the obvious differences; yet, as I will try to suggest later, it may be that Eliot's choice of the realistic novel as the form for her vision is in part an effect, not a cause, of her ambivalent divergences from Wordsworth (for example, a series of her sonnets, which we will consider shortly, articulates these concerns as much as do the novels). Often seeming to intend to, Eliot neither wishes nor is able, as the good sisters invented in Wordsworth's poems are, always to carry out Wordsworthian instructions verbatim. As in Mary Shelley's revision of romanticism in *Frankenstein,* it is precisely the literalness of Eliot's transposition of Wordsworthian themes—her effort to be a docile student on the model of Wordsworth's implied sister—that constitutes her subversion of them.

The Mill on the Floss is Eliot's "most Wordsworthian novel," and it is also her novel most concerned both with female education and with the brother-sister relationship. Maggie Tulliver's experience first as a reader and then as a sister may shed light on Eliot's relation to instruction, especially to brotherly instruction. Maggie's existence in the novel is framed by scenes of her reading. She starts out as an accurate reader who distinguishes easily between elucidating a text foreign to her and inventing her own stories, the two kinds of reading that become confused in Eliot's reading of Wordsworth. Having been reprimanded for her very perceptive reading of *The History of the Devil* as "not quite the right book for a little girl" and asked if she has "no prettier book," Maggie defends herself by opposing accurate reading to invention: "I make stories to the pictures out of my own head, you know." At this point in her story, Maggie feels free both to read independently and to imagine freely, but we see her being chastized as a girl for both processes indifferently. However Maggie reads, "a woman's no business wi' being so clever; it'll turn to trouble, I doubt" (bk. 1, chap. 3).

As Maggie grows up, learning to be feminine, her way of reading changes. As an adolescent in search of spiritual food and guidance, she becomes an overly literal reader of Thomas à Kempis. The eager pupil of two guides, the author and the "quiet hand" that marked certain passages in her second-hand copy, Maggie acts out exactly the text's prescriptions and in so doing radically misreads it in at least two ways. She misconstrues renunciation, not as sorrow, but as an available form of satisfaction, and according to Philip Wakem, she misuses her own gifts: "What you call self-conquest—blinding and deafening yourself to all but one train of impression—is only the culture of monomania in a nature like yours" (bk. 5, chap. 4). The general effect of her reading Thomas à Kempis is to contribute to her education in femininity. She has turned to Thomas à Kempis in the first place because her brother Tom won't let "*my* sister" work to help pay off the family debt, depriving her of any useful (masculine) occupation. Her docility toward the text, her wish to follow its prescriptions exactly, is repeated both in the self-suppression she learns from the text's preaching and in her willingness to let her mother do with her as she pleases: "Her mother felt the change in her with a sort of puzzled wonder that Maggie should be 'growing up so good'; it was amazing that this once 'contrary' child was become so submissive, so backward to assert her own will" (bk. 4, chap. 3). Though Maggie does not think of herself as learning how to be femi-nine—she sees herself as an ascetic—there is a very neat coincidence between her mother's wish for a conventionally good daughter and Thomas à Kempis's message of self-denial.

The more literal her reading, the less accurate and the more feminine. Yet when she attempts, as she used to with the pictures in *The History of the Devil*, her own imaginative departures from Scott's *The Pirate*, which she reads at about the same time, she meets with an equal lack of success that is again part of her education in femininity. Philip offers her his copy of *The Pirate* the first time they meet in the Red Deeps. "O, I began that once," she responds, "I read to where Minna is walking with Cleveland, and I could never get to read the rest. I went on with it in my own head, and I made several endings; but they were all unhappy. I could never make a happy ending out of that beginning" (bk. 5, chap. 1).

Maggie is discovering here the inexorable laws of feminine plotting. It is the same discovery she makes later on when she laments that *Corinne* is merely one more repetition of the law requiring the blonde heroine to triumph over the dark heroine. Her invention of optimistic endings for a love story about a dark-haired girl is limited by the conventions both of plot and of social life. In fact, her endeavor to depart from convention only underscores for her both the heroine's and her own entrapment. Her memory of trying and failing to invent happy endings for *The Pirate* is evoked by the fact that Philip has the book with him because he is studying a scene for a picture. His rationale for offering the book is, "I don't want it now. I shall make a picture of you instead—you, among the Scotch firs and the slanting shadows" (bk. 5, chap. 1). But though she refuses the book, he makes the picture anyway: whether she reads or refuses to read, she will become the static object of a man's vision, in a way that prefigures her final transformation into an object in death.

Maggie enters the novel as a reader, and in her last scene before the flood carries her toward home, Tom, and death, she is reading again, choosing this time between two texts: the letter from Stephen and the words of Thomas à Kempis that would help her resist Stephen's appeal. At this last stage in her growth, her reading is only the passive reiteration of conflicting texts for which she is simply the medium, providing no original words of her own. Ironically, the two texts are really only representations of her own feelings, but she feels that they come from outside her. Stephen's writing is so vivid to her that "she did not *read* the letter: she heard him uttering it, and the voice shook her with its old strange power" (bk. 7, chap. 5). He asks her "Write me one word—say 'Come!' In two days I should be with you." Her response takes the form of writing to his dictation, a literal repetition of his word provoked by the prospect, not of her own joy, but of Stephen's sorrow and by her self-doubts, which "made her once start from her seat to reach the pen and paper, and write 'Come!'" Maggie knows that her obedient and selfless literal repetition is wrong, but she is so exhausted emotionally that she can only wait passively "for the light that would surely come again." When it comes, the corrective to the reiteration of Stephen's word is her repetition of another word: "The words that were marked by the quiet hand in the little old book that she had long ago learned by heart, rushed even to her lips, and found a vent for themselves in a low murmur that was quite lost in the loud driving of the rain against the window." First an unwilling copier of Stephen's word, now a ready voice for the words of Thomas à Kempis, Maggie does at last determine what her own words will be, but they "find no utterance but in a sob," and she defers writing them until the next day, which for her never comes.

Maggie's childhood capacity for original invention and for self-expression has by the end of her story quite vanished. Her adult self is a battleground for conflicting texts; when she takes up a pen or opens her mouth, the words that come forth as if they were her own are not hers. And this state of affairs results from, and in turn reinforces, the self-suppressing submissiveness that is identified throughout as feminine. To learn how to read as a repeater of others' words is feminine, and it is also fatal. Her departures from what she reads as an adolescent (her un-intentional departure from Thomas à Kempis, her effort to vary the inex-orable plot of *The Pirate*) are signs of her vital resistance (willful or unconscious) to feminine submissiveness, even though her efforts fail. When in the last reading scene Maggie gets her texts right, this final docility is a harbinger of her death: her complete passivity as a reader prefigures her succumbing to the flood the next morning.

When Eliot describes her own reading of Wordsworth as a process of possessing herself of what she already possesses, the ambiguous bal-ance of originality and deference prefigures in compressed form some of the features of Maggie's development as a reader. It may be that Eliot is articulating through Maggie the stages of her own education in feminine readership, in how to be a docile or self-suppressing reader. To submit to others' words in Maggie's case is to submit to the law of cause and effect and therefore to reach the unhappy end predicted for all dark her-oines. Eliot thematizes both docility and disobedience to instruction through the relation between Maggie's reading and the pattern of her life: disobedient reading is incompatible with Victorian femininity, yet complete feminine docility leads to the self's silence and ultimately to death. I would like to turn now to some instances of that dual reading in *The Mill on the Floss* and elsewhere that may suggest how the balance between docility and disobedience that Eliot thematizes in Maggie appears in her reading of Wordsworth. How is it possible to honor Wordsworth's words yet not die, as Maggie does, of the desire to be Wordsworth's sister and follow silently and involuntarily the wishes of his words? Carrying out Wordsworth's "remember me" in a way that she asks us to think of as literal (as Maggie's later readings are literal), she nonetheless departs radically from her original in passing from poetic and imaginative vision to the novelist's female vision. But the literal reading that for Maggie results in death issues for Eliot in the novelist's originality.

In calling *The Mill on the Floss* Eliot's most Wordsworthian novel, Donald Stone also locates in it "the most serious case of Wordsworthian blight on Eliot's creative imagination," because "the heroine is paralyzed by a myth of the past and a myth of her own childhood." U. C. Knoepflmacher similarly sees "George Eliot's Wordsworthian novel vainly [trying to] enlist the Romantic's power of memory." As he goes on to point out, where Wordsworth restores himself in "Tintern Abbey" through his own memories and through the memory he makes visible in his sister's eyes, Maggie and Tom succumb to the realities of "evil tongues, / Rash judgments," and the "dreary intercourse of daily life" Wordsworth refers to in his poem (ll. 128–29, 131). The question that these analyses raise is why the myth of the realistic novelist's growth must diverge so radically from Wordsworth's myth of the poet's growth. "Tintern Abbey" and "Nutting" have only an incidental place for the sister, whereas the poet's accounts of the growth of the imagination picture a solitary, even narcissistic relation between himself and nature's maternal presence in childhood. At its most powerful, too, the visionary imagination can shut out the ordinary, visible world, as Dorothy Wordsworth sees in the "spots of time" and the Simplon Pass passages in *The Prelude*. Eliot's myth of childhood, however, for reasons that I will explore more fully later on, necessarily includes other people and a visible world that can never be ignored. In her revision of the Wordsworthian myth, Eliot's most autobiographical characters pass through what appears to be Wordsworthian childhoods, not to become romantic poets, but to find that their ideal childhood visions are thwarted by circumstances or by social needs. This revision closely resembles the literalizations in *Wuthering Heights, Jane Eyre,* and *Frankenstein,* all of which, in different ways, distort a romantic ideal. Eliot sets her heroines' insatiable need for love, together with her own narrative commitment to realism, against the antisocial implications of what she represents as the introverting power of the imagination. Her heroines' need for love is insatiable because those who can supply it never love as unconditionally as Wordsworth's nature does, and Eliot schools her heroines to choose a love that represents a turning away from disruptive visionary power. In *The Mill on the Floss* and in the lesser-known sonnet sequence "Brother and Sister" (1869), the heroine gives up visionary aspirations (that are perhaps in any case untenable in the world of the novel) in favor of the love of a usually more practical-minded brother that makes childhood last forever and closes off the visionary world. That choice may lead to death, but the loss of vision may also be compensated for by an increase in wisdom ultimately more appropriate to the novel than to poetry.

This ambivalent relation to Wordsworth stands out in one of the moments considered most Wordsworthian in Eliot, the fishing scene in *The Mill on the Floss* and the narrator's subsequent reflections on the value of memories of a childhood passed in nature (bk. 1, chap. 5). A close look at these passages reveals a willful misreading of the Wordsworthian implications of the scene, and the later consequences of the scene are the opposite of Wordsworthian. Opposing one brother (Tom) to a very different one (Wordsworth, brother of silent sisters), Eliot has Maggie defend against Wordsworth's authority while retaining all the forms of a sister's deference.

As Sandra Gilbert and Susan Gubar point out, Maggie and Tom spend most of their precious time together making each other miserable, and while Maggie, Tom, and their narrator cling to the idea that their idyllic fishing expedition is typical of their childhood, the reader must suspect the effort to generalize from this exceptional scene. The children live in a fallen, gendered world in which they can never escape for very long the pain produced by their social condition. Fishing harmoniously together at "the old favourite spot," "Maggie thought it would make a very nice heaven to sit by the pool in that way, and never be scolded." But this heaven is brief and contingent on absolute physical and mental seclusion. That it cannot be carried over into the common day of their ordinary lives is underscored by the very precise description of its locale. The "old favourite spot" is a pool of unknown depth and mysterious origin that is literally hidden from view, being "framed in with willows and tall reeds, so that the water was only to be seen when you got close to the brink."

Tom supervises the practical business of fishing, but Maggie "had forgotten all about the fish, and was looking dreamily at the glassy water." Hearing Tom's "loud whisper," Maggie is "frightened lest she had been doing something wrong, as usual," and when it turns out instead that she had inadvertently caught a fish, she is "not conscious of unusual merit." Maggie's happiness consists in such additional absence of wrongdoing and in listening alternately to Tom's whispers and to the "happy whisperings" exchanged between the "light dipping sounds of the rising fish" and the gentle rustling of the willows and reeds. These illusions of reciprocity—for she and Tom communicate no more effectively than the water and the willows—encourage the children's equally illusory idea that their lives will always be like this. The narrator ends her account of Maggie and Tom by generalizing the Wordsworthian principle that the scene has apparently generated: "Life did change for Tom and Maggie; and yet they were not wrong in believing that the thoughts and loves of these first years would always make part of their lives." The narrator then turns to generalize about all human childhoods and finally speaks of her own.

It would seem at this point that "the thoughts and loves of these first years" refers primarily to the children's love for each other, with the mill and the river as setting. But as the passage continues into its larger and explicitly Wordsworthian frame of reference, the reader is given the strange impression that the foregoing scene has instead been solely concerned with the children's love for their natural surroundings.

> We could never have loved the earth so well if we had had no childhood in it,—if it were not the earth where the same flowers come up again every spring that we used to gather with our tiny fingers as we sat lisping to ourselves on the grass. . . . What novelty is worth that sweet monotony where everything is known, and *loved* because it is known?

The child's love of "rural objects" leads here, not to deeper, wider kinds of love, but simply to a renewed love of those identical objects. Even the expected reference to the endurance of Maggie's love for Tom—for which there would in any case be no place in the Wordsworthian paradigm of a solitary childhood in nature—is replaced by this love of objects. Stressing continuity over growth, the passage suggests how the Wordsworthian features of Maggie's childhood will contribute to narrowing her consciousness, not enlarging it. When, seeing all their old possessions taken away after the bankruptcy, Maggie cries to Tom, "The end of our lives will have nothing in it like the beginning!" (bk. 3, chap. 6), Eliot is presenting us with a version of childhood far more literal than Wordsworth's.

Eliot's ambiguous expression "make part of their lives" suggests, vaguely enough so as not to appear purposely misleading, the Wordsworthian idea that the experiences of childhood seed the ground of character to bear unpredictable fruits, as when Wordsworth's "glad animal movements," remembered later, lead circuitously to the more sober pleasures of the mature poet. He recalls specific incidents from his childhood for their place in his growing awareness, first of nature's presence and then of his own mind's powers. But Maggie's yearnings later are for particular objects—this book, this mill, that river—and in this she is not altogether different from the literal-minded Tom, whose adult energies are devoted solely to repossessing his property, or even from her even more limited mother, whose worship of objects connected with her Dodson past is pathetic and un-Wordsworthian in the extreme. For Maggie, objects loved in childhood remain beloved for their own sakes, or for their place in consecrating her love for her brother, but never for what they teach her about the growth of her own mind. A literal recapitulation of childhood could hardly be further from Wordsworth's aims for himself as a poet; he does portray the dangers of obsessive fixation to a particular spot, but only in characters like Margaret in *The Excursion,* never in images of himself. Within the cultural tradition that can be summarized as the symbolic order, as we have seen [elsewhere], daughters may view objects, or the literal, more favorably than do sons, both through training and through inclination based on early childhood; but where the transcendence of all things is valued, objects are devalued. Eliot, sharing her heroine's love of things, yet recognizing the cost of this love within the symbolic order, identifies growth with transcendence and regression and death with the literal.

The Mill on the Floss's largest plot patterns turn on Maggie's continual need to reaffirm her ties to home. Her conflicting loves for Tom and for Philip are almost equally strong, having taken root in kindnesses conferred in childhood. Among her first sensations on "waking" from "the great temptation" is the urgent need to go home, where she may affirm her identity as a child needing discipline and protection from her wilder impulses and her adult self. The feature of childhood she wishes to repeat is not its illusion of Edenic peace but its pain: "In her anguish at the injury she had inflicted—she almost desired to endure the severity of Tom's reproof, to submit in patient silence to that harsh disapproving judgment against which she had so often rebelled" (bk. 7, chap. 1). She craves and believes she can return to a pattern, established in childhood by incidents like those with Tom's rabbits or the jam puffs, of harsh judgment, confession, and forgiveness: "I will endure anything. I want to be kept from doing wrong again." Tom, refusing her home and forgiveness, refuses to let her be a child again. But her final attempt to return to the mill (on the flood) does succeed in achieving a restoration both of childhood ties and of cathartic pain. Her death in returning home is thus doubly ensured: what she wants from childhood is its pain, and her wish to turn backward to childhood is, like Cathy's in *Wuthering Heights,* a death wish.

For Wordsworth, the natural objects to which the child feels bonded are always subordinate to the bond itself and to the wider sense of connectedness and vitality engendered by that bond, but Maggie's loyalty does not shift from those primary objects themselves. Wordsworth grows past his love for his mother and even for nature's material presence, but Maggie never transcends her love for Tom. Wordsworth's memories of childhood in *The Prelude* even include "the impressive discipline of fear" (bk. 1, l. 603) brought by nature's "Severer interventions, ministry / More palpable" (bk. 1, ll. 355–56). (Quotations from *The Prelude* are from the 1850 version.) But where Wordsworth's memory transforms that pain into imaginative power, Maggie seeks a literal recapitulation of the identical pain (inflicted in the same home by the same person) in Tom's punishment. The huge fragments of machinery that overtake Maggie and Tom in the flood are literalization itself: the failure of a life's worth of experiences to transcend themselves, remaining instead an agglomeration of things—the very literalness of the novel's revision of the Wordsworthian pattern. The narrator's conclusion to the fishing episode, speaking of the "sweet monotony" of a well-known landscape and of the return of the seasons, offers a seductively beautiful version of the narrative pattern of Maggie's life. In both, what might be self-transcendent turns out to be a return to particularity. Maggie's repetitions transform the beautiful "sweet monotony" into something more dangerous, since to repeat, within the terms of the symbolic order, is to regress, and to regress is to die.

To answer the question of why neither Maggie nor her narrative can go, or even want to go, beyond the literal, it may be useful at this point to suggest the relationship between Maggie's education in feminine reading and her literalizing life. Along with her regressive wishes, her reading prefigures, if it does not actually ensure, her death. When Maggie cries out "the end of our lives will have nothing in it like the beginning," her immediate reference is to the copy of *The Pilgrim's Progress* that she interpreted so acutely for Mr. Riley in the first reading scene. "'Our dear old Pilgrim's Progress that you coloured with your little paints; and that picture of Pilgrim with a mantle on, looking just like a turtle—oh dear!' Maggie went on, half sobbing as she turned over the few books. 'I thought we should never part with that while we lived'" (bk. 3, chap. 6). Pilgrim "looking just like a turtle" reminds us that this book symbolizes her independent way in childhood of "making stories to the pictures out of [her] own head," a way of reading that is now lost to her. When the book is sold off with all the other books, it is converted into the chief symbol, among the objects that Maggie misses, of her literalization of the Wordsworthian sense of the past and thus of the kind of literal reading into which she has now fallen. Furthermore, it is Maggie's sorrow over the loss of the book that indirectly leads her to become a more and more literal reader: it is because of witnessing her sorrow that Bob Jakin later brings Maggie the gift of assorted books among which she finds the Thomas à Kempis. Her docile feminine repetitions, first of Stephen's "Come!" and then of the memorized text of Thomas à Kempis, echo and confirm her desire to repeat her childhood by returning home to Tom and the mill, first after she has left Stephen and finally during the flood, a passive repetition that overdetermines her death. These repetitions of texts represent an abandonment of self that signals the approach of death; and that the repetition is literal prefigures the particular shape that the death will take—her being overtaken by the huge mass of machinery on the flood. This machinery recalls the "machinery of a story" into which Shelley literalizes romantic texts, with monstrous consequences that are no less fatal than those of the machinery that overtakes Maggie. Her reading acts do not themselves cause Maggie's death, but they identify the thematics of return and of love of the literal with rhetorical repetition, and they identify the thematics of death with the lack of one's own word. And as specifically feminine reading acts, they identify learned feminine behavior with return, literal repetition, death, and silence.

Maggie's docility and final silence connect her, then, to the figure Wordsworth projects of his silent, listening sister. Yet her kind of education is also linked to Wordsworth's own. The sonnet sequence "Brother and Sister" presents another version of Maggie's kind of education, one that displays some verbal similarity to a Wordsworthian scene of the poet's instruction. Drawn from the same stock of Eliot's own experience as the dreamy little sister of a practical-minded older brother, the sonnet sequence shares with the fishing scene in *The Mill on the Floss* both its general contours of plot and characterization and its ostensible aim to assert that "the thoughts and loves of these first years would always make part of their lives." The sonnet sequence also revises the rowing episode from book 1 of *The Prelude,* which Eliot had reread at least two years previous to composing the sonnets and perhaps more recently than that. In order to find a paradigm more suitable than that of the silent sister, Eliot considers the future poet; yet she cannot go so far as to portray herself as a brother. Remaining a sister, she makes clear the limits that gender places on what it is possible for a heroine to do or to be.

Like the round pool, the canal setting of the sonnets' fishing episode literalizes the sublime. Where the round pool is both profound and obscure, "Our brown canal was endless to my thought," and barges float into view around "a grassy hill to me sublime / With some Unknown beyond it" (sonnet 6). While the brother and sister fish together in the canal, the sister tells us that "One day my brother left me in high charge, / To mind the rod while he went seeking bait" (sonnet 7), with instructions to pull the line out of the way of oncoming barges. Like Maggie fishing in the round pool, the little sister's attention lapses,

> Till sky and earth took on a strange new light
> And seemed a dream-world floating on some tide—
> A fair pavilioned boat for me alone
> Bearing me onward through the vast unknown.

Her "dreamy peace" is broken by the arrival of a barge and by the sounds of her brother's anger, but the unhappy situation is turned around when it appears that the line she lifts out at the last minute has a fish on it, so that her "guilt that won the prey" is "Now turned to merit" (sonnet 8). This scene replays very closely Maggie's fishing scene, in which she, too, felt "she had been doing something wrong, as usual," but has instead by pure chance caught a fish. Like Maggie, the little sister here, accidentally rewarded for doing wrong, learns from this event only that "luck was with glory wed." Morally ambiguous, these scenes teach Maggie and the little sister the insignificance of their actions relative to material coincidence.

Like the two fishing scenes, Wordsworth's rowing episode in book 1 of *The Prelude* concerns a child's transgression, but Wordsworth's "act of stealth / And troubled pleasure" (ll. 361–62) clearly deserves and as clearly receives punishment, unlike the ambiguous moral situations in which the two little girls find themselves. Having stolen a rowboat, Wordsworth's child enjoys a brief period of wonder that may be identified with what Coleridge and Wordsworth call "fancy." The "elfin pinnance" moves on,

> Leaving behind her still, on either side,
> Small circles glittering idly in the moon,
> Until they melted all into one track
> Of sparkling light.
>
> (ll. 364–67)

This part of the episode corresponds to the "dreamy peace" that appears sublime for the sister in the sonnets, a remembered state that includes a vision of "The wondrous watery rings that died too soon" (sonnet 6), and corresponds also to the moment of transgression before transgression is recognized as such, when "sky and earth took on a strange new light / And seemed a dream-world." The scene turns sinister for Wordsworth's child when, as he rows away from the shore, "the stars and the grey sky" beyond the ridge are replaced by "a huge peak, black and huge" that "As if with voluntary power instinct / Upreared its head" and that appears to grow larger and to stride after him as the boy tries to escape it (ll. 372, 378–80). This huge and animated peak corresponds in sonnet 8 to the "barge's pitch-black prow" appearing around the hill that—like Wordsworth's ridge, beyond which is only the sky—has previously seemed a sublime vacancy.

Despite the similarity of the two situations, the moral outcome is entirely different for each child. Where Wordsworth senses that nature has arranged this spectacle for his instruction, the looming object is for Eliot an accidental occurrence, not the product of a moral design. The actual barge might be the literalization of the little girl's dream of the "fair pavilioned boat," so that its frightening arrival would be the self-inflicted punishment for daydreaming, as Wordsworth's "huge peak, black and huge" seems to embody the boy's guilt. But the barge in the sonnets is pursuing its own independent, commercial course—unknown to the girl and not therefore a product of her imagination—and does not "str[i]de after" her in the manner of the purposeful "grim shape" of Wordsworth's story. Its arrival is simply bad luck, just as the appearance of the fish on her line at the critical moment is simply good luck. Both are material accidents occurring independently of the girl's psychic growth. Significantly, Eliot's child is stationary on the canal bank, a passive spectator in a world of powerful things that are governed by chance. Of course, if we look at what actually happens in Wordsworth, the appearance of the peak on the horizon is sheer accident too. What is important is that while the girl knows that she is subject to luck, the boy never deviates from his certainty that, because nature regulates her actions according to the needs of his education, nature has in this instance acted for him.

Had the girl been punished for daydreaming, by losing the line, say, she would have received an amply ambiguous moral lesson against imaginative, rather than immoral (as for Wordsworth), actions. As it is, she is even more confusingly rewarded by not being punished for doing something that is considered wrong. Out of this confusion, if there is any lesson for her, it is that daydreaming is inefficacious and irrelevant, too trivial to be either punished or rewarded. Yet it is precisely at this point in the story that Wordsworth's child's imagination is made to grow. One of nature's "severer interventions" on his behalf issues first and almost incidentally in a moral lesson that is both clear and just, a lesson that is, however, subordinate to the deep and troubling indeterminacy he feels in response to his discovery of nature's ministrations:

> my brain
> Worked with a dim and undetermined sense
> Of unknown modes of being; o'er my thoughts
> There hung a darkness, call it solitude
> Or blank desertion.
>
> (ll. 391–95)

This "blank desertion" suspends and restructures the boy's total relation to the world around him. Lacking nature's active ministry, Eliot's child learns both to fear and to discount her imagination.

Following the fishing episode, the little sister completes her conversion from dreaming by entering into her brother's exclusively physical pleasures, such as knocking apples out of trees and playing with marbles and tops.

> Grasped by such fellowship my vagrant thought
> Ceased with dream-fruit dream-wishes to fulfill
> My aëry-picturing fantasy was taught
> Subjection to the harder, truer skill
>
> That seeks with deeds to grave a thought-tracked line
> And by "What is," "What will be" to define.
>
> (sonnet 10)

This conversion to the principles of linear plot and realism is presented as good, supported by and reinforcing the myth of George Eliot as a contentedly realistic novelist, even though the examples of realistic behavior she adduces are not very persuasive. The next (and final) sonnet's sketch of the two children's futures confirms the realist's patterning of "What will be" on "What is," when "the dire years whose awful name is Change" "pitiless" shapes their souls "in two forms that range / Two elements which sever their life's course" (sonnet 11). Eliot is formulating here in terms that seem applicable to herself as a realistic novelist the same discovery that Maggie makes when she tries to invent alternate endings for the heroine in *The Pirate*. "I could never make a happy ending out of that beginning" is Maggie's recognition that, like Minna, she will succumb to the inexorable laws of cause and effect of realistic plotting.

The sonnets' commitment to linear plotting reverses Wordsworth's conclusion to the rowing scene. Moving from the actual "huge peak, black and huge" to the "huge and mighty forms" of the mind, Wordsworth concludes with a disruption between the familiar past and any possible future, a cleavage that is the signature of the imagination:

> No familiar shapes
> Remained, no pleasant images of trees,
> Of sea or sky, no colours of green fields;
> But huge and mighty forms, that do not live
> Like living men, moved slowly through the mind
> By day, and were a trouble to my dreams.
> (ll. 395–400)

Wordsworth does value familiar shapes and rural images, but ultimately because they aid in forming and sustaining the affections of the heart, which then can survive independently of shapes and images. The imagination casts off, if painfully, precisely those things that both Maggie and the narrator of *The Mill on the Floss* cling to and affirm to be of highest value in themselves. While Wordsworth moves from actual sight to figurative vision, Eliot moves in the opposite direction, from figure (Wordsworth's text) to thing. The sonnets' turn to realism and the asserted determination of the future by the present reiterates both Maggie's suffocating repetitions of the past and the way in which the novel's narrator, moving at the close of the fishing scene, like Maggie, not from the finite to the sublime but from particular to particular, recalls and celebrates the literal repetition of exactly those "familiar shapes," those "pleasant images of trees, / Of sea or sky," those "colours of green fields" that Wordsworth's young imagination in its most powerful activity discards. For the narrator, love of a natural scene leads beautifully but statically to love of the same natural scene:

> These familiar flowers, these well-remembered bird-notes, this sky, with its fitful brightness, these furrowed and grassy fields, each with a sort of personality given to it by the capricious hedgerows—such things as these are the mother tongue of our imagination, the language that is laden with all the subtle inextricable associations the fleeting hours of our childhood left behind them. Our delight in the sunshine on the deep-bladed grass to-day, might be no more than the faint perception of wearied souls, if it were not for the sunshine and the grass in the far-off years which still live in us, and transform our perception into love.
>
> (bk. 1, chap. 5)

The allusion to the imagination is problematic here, since this love, rich as it is, is not what Wordsworth, whose presence is so clearly invoked, would call the imagination. Human relatedness stands in the place of Wordsworth's solitary perception of nature as the central formative influence on the growing child. Prefatory to the series of related incidents that culminates in the rowing episode, Wordsworth writes: "Fair seed-time had my soul, and I grew up / Fostered alike by beauty and by fear" (ll. 301–2). In a comparable position prefatory to the fishing incident, Eliot recalls Wordsworth's lines, but with a crucial difference:

> Thus rambling we were schooled in deepest lore,
> And learned the meanings that give words a soul,
> The fear, the love, the primal passionate store,
>
> . . . .
>
> Those hours were seed to all my after good.
>
> (sonnet 5)

Wordsworth's beauty and fear are nature's ministries, devoted gratuitously and unconditionally to the growing boy, while for Eliot "the fear, the love" are purely human. The love is between the sister and the brother, and the fear is merely of its loss (and also of a gypsy glimpsed in the sonnet preceding these lines). Just as throughout *The Mill on the Floss* Maggie's "need of love had triumphed over her pride, . . . it is a wonderful subduer, this need of love" (bk. 1, chap. 5), the little sister's allegiance to realism results from a kind of emotional blackmail through which her other needs as an individual are subordinated to the one overwhelming craving to be loved. The sister purchases love through acknowledging the preeminence of the objects that the brother loves. The transformation of perception into love defines the imagination as a binding love (of things and of the brother inextricably) that for Maggie will become obsessive and constricting and that for Wordsworth is antithetical to the imagination.

That "things" should have so privileged a relation to the imagination is troubling, but that things should be "the mother tongue of our imagination" is more problematic still, as the phase ironically illuminates one source of Eliot's heroines' exclusive need to choose love over the world of imagination. A "mother tongue" in Wordsworth might signify feminized nature's fostering of imaginative growth in passages such as the rowing episode, a fostering made possible by the myth of the mother's early disappearance and replacement by figurative substitutes. But the nature for which Eliot's narrator expresses her enduring love is not at all Wordsworth's maternal nature but rather the nature of objects that signify the brother's realism and the sister's devotion to it. Because of the girl's differing place in and experience of the family configuration, it would be impossible for any female character in Eliot ever to imagine herself in the same relation to the idea of maternal nature that Wordsworth is privileged to feel. As in *Jane Eyre* and *Wuthering Heights,* the mother in Eliot would repeal, not encourage, her daughter's entry into the symbolic order, an entry about which Eliot appears to feel some ambivalence. Mrs. Tulliver's restrictiveness toward Maggie, her partiality to Tom, and her preoccupation with domestic objects reappear in the mother in "Brother and Sister," whose loving overprotectiveness the children try to escape: "Our mother bade us keep the trodden ways," while "the benediction of her gaze / Clung to us lessening, and pursued us still" (sonnet 3). In a social world in which mothers are not "presences" but socially conditioned beings, these little sisters are unable to assume nature's figuratively maternal love and guidance in the way that Wordsworth's young self can, and no other, more specifically female, relation to the mother can be valued instead.

Wordsworth's introduction to the rowing episode, "One summer evening (led by her)" (l. 357), emphasizes the theme of nature's purposive moral instruction. Introducing her comparable story in "Brother and Sister," Eliot writes, "One day my brother left me in high charge." It is under the brother's responsibility that the girl experiences the moral confusion of luck. The brother can hardly regulate circumstances as nature can, and he cannot be expected to direct the event toward his sister's moral growth. His love, like almost any human love after the myth of maternal love, is conditional, almost as accidental as the motions of barges and fish, and can never be taken for granted by his sister. Lacking the unconditional devotion of the reinvented mother, daughters in Eliot seek for the imagination a *brother* tongue. But because of the brother's fixation on objects that seal him, together with the sister who accepts his values, away from the imagination, that tongue is unobtainable. The transformation of perception into love prevents the transformation of perception into the Wordsworthian, visionary imagination.

In the rowing episode, the boy must violate the law in order to learn of nature's ceaseless attention to his actions, just as in "Nutting" the boy must ravage the virgin bower before he can discover that "there is a spirit in the woods." Such experiences are necessary to the boy's moral and imaginative education, and they are never final because maternal nature always forgives. It is these experiences from which Wordsworth as a brother would protect his sister. Eliot's young sisters are just as much protected from experiencing such enlarging transgressions by their fear of losing the brother's love. The two kinds of brothers (Wordsworth, on the one hand and Tom and the brother of the sonnets on the other) share this trait of mediating, or attempting to, between their younger sisters and the sublime. They are linked only in this regard, standing otherwise for opposing values, but this connection suggests the significance of their opposition in Eliot's alignment of them.

Eliot's comments about reading Wordsworth, we have seen, like the change in Maggie's reading, reflect an ambivalent response to the authority of a text that seems both to foster and to subvert their originality. The temptation to silence or rote repetition is an especially feminine one, a temptation to docility and self-suppression. Thus though Eliot might like to write in congruence with a revered male authority, conforming as Wordsworth's silent sister might do, or as Maggie does in devoutly repeating the words of Thomas à Kempis, she cannot and does not want to do so in these gendered matters. To defend against being Wordsworth's sister (and perhaps in part also because Mary Ann Evans had such a brother), Eliot represents her heroines as sisters of explicitly anti-Wordsworthian brothers, so that to follow the authority of one is necessarily to contravene that of the other. Excluded from the Wordsworthian paradigm for continuity between a childhood spent with a guiding maternal nature and visionary imagination, Eliot and her female characters seek approval in brothers. But they find that the brother's approval is earned only by turning away from what the other brother, Wordsworth, would approve, the solitary world of the imagination, toward a world governed by the law of cause and effect. When Eliot's heroines are torn between the imaginary world of Wordsworth and the practical world of the other brothers, they thematize the tension between Eliot's desire to listen silently to or repeat Wordsworth and her desire to show that what she reads in his authoritative texts was originally her own. To have the heroine enter fully into the world of imagination would be to concur that there are no truths beyond Wordsworth's, while to have her wholly allied with the brother would be, for Eliot, to deny altogether the values she shares with Wordsworth. Defending herself from one powerful male authority by inventing (or trusting) another, Eliot finds a way to be at once original and deferential.

To repeat Wordsworth literally would in any case be a contradiction in terms. Eliot exploits this contradiction fully: to pay proper homage to Wordsworth would be to have him speak through her, as Maggie lets Thomas à Kempis speak through her; but to do so is necessarily to get Wordsworth wrong and thus to fail to pay proper homage. The more literally Maggie repeats the texts authoritative for her, and the more literally Eliot has her live out what seem to be Wordsworthian notions (in her repetitions of childhood experiences and in her desire for the home objects), the closer she comes both to perfect femininity and to death. But the more literal the repetition, the more divergent from, and subversive of, Wordsworth's aims, for to read Wordsworth literally in a female context is to become a realist. Where the Wordsworthian imagination interrupts or would interrupt between "What is" and "What will be," between material cause and effect, and between the introduction of a dark heroine and the certainty that her end will be unhappy, Eliot's heroines, in submitting to these laws, define a realistic fictional world. The literalizing that characterizes Maggie's adult feelings and actions (her love of the home objects, her desire for literal repetitions of her early life, and her repetitions of texts) is paralleled by Eliot's general turn toward what she persuades us is realism. For Maggie, literalization leads to her death, but it leads for Eliot to something definitively her own—her identity as a novelist of real life and of female experience, an identity that she establishes under cover of seeming to be a docile, feminine reader of her beloved Wordsworth. It is in fact Maggie's death that consolidates Eliot's vital independence from Wordsworth: Maggie dies of choosing social bonds over the self's needs. The scenes of Maggie's reading and instruction are also the scenes of Eliot's reading and instruction; but while Maggie fatally learns the lesson of feminine readership, Eliot fortunately fails.

In later novels, Eliot continues the exploration we have observed in *The Mill on the Floss* of the consequences of literalizing Wordsworthian vision both for her heroines and for her own practice as an author. In the earlier novel, she frames as painfully as possible the price of Maggie's inevitable and female literalizations, and she distinguishes between the fatal effects on Maggie of her passive reading and the critique the author is able to make, through Maggie's suffering, of her own reading. In *Middlemarch*, however, she gives what emerges as the cause of Maggie's suffering a somewhat more comic turn, and she comes closer to identifying her own practices of reading and writing with those of her characters. After emblematically Wordsworthian childhoods, both Mary Garth and Dorothea Brooke give up what are represented as visionary aspirations in favor of the love of (if not a brother, as in Maggie's case) a lover who is like a brother, whose love makes childhood last forever and closes off the visionary world. At the same time, it is as the epigraph to chapter 57 of *Middlemarch* that Eliot writes one of her most important accounts of the relation between her writing and prior texts, an account that suggests both her mastery of concealing subversive reading within apparent docility and her claim that that mastery was always already accomplished, as it is here situated in childhood.

The epigraph consists of a sonnet:

> They numbered scarce eight summers when a name
> Rose on their souls and stirred such motions there
> As thrill the buds and shape their hidden frame
> At penetration of the quickening air:
> His name who told of loyal Evan Dhu,
> Of quaint Bradwardine, and Vich Ian Vor,
> Making the little world their childhood knew
> Large with a land of mountain, lake, and scaur,
> And larger yet with wonder, love, belief
> Toward Walter Scott, who living far away
> Sent them this wealth of joy and noble grief.
> The book and they must part, but day by day,
> In lines that thwart like portly spiders ran,
> They wrote the tale, from Tully Veolan.

Immersed in a copy of *Waverley* loaned to her sister and returned before she could finish it, Mary Ann's response to her loss was to "write out" the part of the story she had read. Neither the sonnet nor the anecdote makes it clear how creative or repetitive this writing was. In the high-toned letter to Maria Lewis in which she repents of her early guilty penchant for novel reading, she says that from her dissatisfaction with the world around her "I was constantly living in a world of my own creation," for which novels supplied "the materials . . . for building my castles in the air." Did her reading of *Waverley* provide the impetus for her own inventions, as she suggests in this letter? Or did she, clinging faithfully to memory, literally record the same story that she had read? "Wrote the tale" suggests something that defies the opposition between these two possibilities: she may have so fully internalized Scott as to have been able to reproduce his story feeling that it was her own. Openly venerating Scott, eight-year-old Mary Ann nonethelsss retained both her freedom to build castles in the air and her authority over Scott; "wrote the tale" suggests that she wrote Scott as well as Scott himself could have.

This mixture of veneration and independence in one literary act contrasts with the situation of Maggie, for whom there is an abrupt disjunction between reading as invention—as when she "makes stories to the pictures out of [her] own head" as a child, or when later she wishes vainly to change the ending of *The Pirate*—and her reading as rote repetition, as when in a trance of submissiveness at the end of her life she murmurs the words of Thomas à Kempis. The situation in the *Middlemarch* sonnet also contrasts to another act of literary transmission, the acting out with bow and arrows of Scott's archery scene in *Ivanhoe* by Mary Garth's little brother, Ben, in the chapter of which the sonnet is the epigraph. During the reading out loud of the scene, "Ben . . . was making himself dreadfully disagreeable, Letty thought, by begging all present to observe his random shots, which no one wished to do." The little-boy egotism of Ben's reading, which would altogether replace the original text, in its contrast to the more docile listening of the little sister, Letty, suggests that gender matters again in the difference between his awkward aggressiveness and the subtler mastery of the writer in the sonnet. The writing of the tale in the sonnet seems indeed most closely to resemble Eliot's own practice with respect to Wordsworth, in that following open veneration of an authoritative male original, and after dutifully repeating the beginning of his story, both Mary Ann and Eliot change the ending to suit their own requirements, concealing the extent of the change. This is true of Eliot's practice in *The Mill on the Floss,* as we have seen, and it is also true of *Middlemarch.* But while Eliot expresses her sense of the cost and difficulty of such a practice and perhaps protests the necessity of it through Maggie's suffering, the fact that she makes Dorothea's and Mary's inevitably docile female departures from a Wordsworthian original so much less painful than Maggie's suggests that her own departures do not so much protest as accept and even celebrate what can be done within the limits of Victorian womanly duty.

Although we have treated "Brother and Sister" as an adjunct to *The Mill on the Floss,* it was written several years later. Eliot seems to have written "Brother and Sister" in part to revise the use in *The Mill on the Floss* of childhood memories of her brother and of nature, but the more immediate occasion of its composition may have been *Middlemarch.* Memories of her childhood with Isaac may have come back to Eliot with special vividness, as Gordon Haight suggests, because at that time she was beginning to construct the world of Middlemarch in the Warwickshire of her childhood. The writing of *Middlemarch,* as it was first conceived, began in the summer of 1869 with "the Vincy and Featherstone parts"—original versions of all or parts of what are now chapters 11 through 14—and with an "introduction," probably a version of the account of Lydgate's early life, including his "intellectual passion," that the present chapter 15 comprises. Eliot wrote "Brother and Sister" in July 1869; on July 19 she notes in her journal that she is "writing an introduction to 'Middlemarch,'" and on August 2, she writes that she has begun with the Vincy and Featherstone parts. (This writing all takes place well before the composition of Dorothea's story and the even later integration of that story into *Middlemarch.*) Among "the various elements of the story [that] have been soliciting [her] mind for years—asking for a complete embodiment," she notes in February 1869, Fred Vincy and Mary Garth (then named Mary Dove) must have solicited almost the most effectively. "Brother and Sister" recasts the story of Maggie and Tom, and Fred and Mary in turn inherit that theme of a love that because it begins in childhood is unalterable and is associated with an attachment to the land. In developing this relationship, Eliot continues to set the childhood experience of love and of nature in opposition to the growth of what might become the faculty of imagination. As in the brother and sister relationships in *The Mill on the Floss* and the sonnet sequence, although she invokes the authorizing presence of the Wordsworthian pattern, she sees a determining difference between children who grow up in male-female pairs and Wordsworth's specifically male child, whose richest experiences take place in a solitude shared only by the maternal nature of his invention.

Like that of the sisters and brothers, Fred's and Mary's love for each other refers ever backward to an imagined Eden of original, perfect love. They were constant playfellows as children, and "Fred at six years old thought [Mary] the nicest girl in the world, making her his wife with a brass ring which he had cut from an umbrella" (chap. 23). Later when Farebrother, sent by Fred, is trying to find out the state of Mary's affections, Mary thinks (or the indirect discourse suggests that she thinks) back to that early betrothal, and she explains, "It has taken such deep root in me—my gratitude to him for always loving me best, and minding so much if I hurt myself, from the time when we were very little. I cannot imagine any new feeling coming to make that weaker" (chap. 52). (Maggie and the little sister also value protectiveness, as Mary does here, although the brothers' protection takes more often the form of a painful restraint than the more promising form of "minding so much.")

Fred's "expectations" about Stone Court are a comic version of Maggie and Tom's attachment to their father's mill, but they occupy functionally the same place, in that they demand a return to a specific piece of land, a demand that is fulfilled, if not in precisely the manner Fred had anticipated. Although of all the major characters in the novel Mary alone never forms any wish or plan, she is delighted when her father's new job allows her to refuse a teaching job and stay home. Very early in our introduction to the Fred and Mary plot, before we have even met Mary, a Wordsworthian passage about love for a landscape familiar from childhood established that their story is rooted to the land:

> Little details gave each field particular physiognomy, dear to the eyes that have looked on them from childhood: the pool in the corner where the grasses were dank and trees leaned whisperingly; the great oak shadowing a bare place in mid-pasture. . . . These are the things that make the gamut of joy in landscape to midland-bred souls—the things they toddled among, or perhaps learned by heart standing between their father's knees while he drove leisurely.
>
> (chap. 12)

The passage—whose pool and whispering trees we may recognize from *The Mill on the Floss*—has no direct bearing on the immediate feelings of Fred and Rosamond, who are riding through this landscape on their way to Stone Court. Although Fred is visiting Featherstone to work on his chances for an inheritance, the passage promises that Fred may have a deeper love for the land, a promise fulfilled later by his pleasure in working with Caleb Garth and by his eventual possession of Stone Court as a careful farmer, not as a capitalist. Rosamond's relation to the passage is wholly ironic: her visit to Stone Court is motivated by her wish to meet the new young doctor, who interests her because, as opposed to Fred's attachment to his old playfellow, "She was tired of the faces and figures she had always been used to—the various irregular profiles and gaits and turns of phrase distinguishing those Middlemarch young men whom she had known as boys" (chap. 11).

The variable disjunctiveness between the Wordsworthian passage and the characters to whom it appears immediately to apply is reinforced by manuscript evidence that the passage was written after the scene it precedes. The visit to Stone Court was among those passages written before August 2, 1869, although the extant manuscript may be a later and possibly revised copy, but the introductory paragraph on the landscape belongs to a section added after Eliot had dropped *Middlemarch,* written "Miss Brooke," and then decided to join the two stories. Although the passage may have had an original in the manuscript of 1869, as it now stands it is part of a section added as a bridge, and in fact the chapter does read as though the first paragraph were tacked on to it. Like the Wordsworthian revery at the close of the fishing scene in *The Mill on the Floss,* and despite later intimations of similar themes in Fred and Mary's story (or perhaps because of them), the passage calls attention to itself as not quite fitting its context, as if Eliot were artifically suggesting Wordsworthian possibilities that do not emerge organically from the story.

The same disjunction that occurs between this landscape passage and the story adjacent to it reappears on a larger scale in the relation between Fred and Mary's story and the rest of the novel. Fred and Mary's story was apparently the most difficult for Eliot to interweave with the other plots. In her journal for March 1871, she worried that she had "too much matter" for the novel—"to many 'momenti'"—and Jerome Beaty conjectures that only loyalty to her original conception of the book (her own excessive bond to the childhood of the book) kept her from discarding the Fred-Mary plot, which does very little to bridge the separately conceived stories of Lydgate and Dorothea. The introduction in progress in July 1869—if it was the prototype of the present chapter 15—was about Lydgate's "intellectual passion" for anatomy, formed in childhood, resistant to change, and compared (at least in the final version) specifically to romantic passion. Eliot may have originally conceived the novel as the juxtaposition of these two childhood passions. The decision to incorporate Dorothea's story into *Middlemarch* meant a shift in focus from themes shared by Lydgate's story and by Fred and Mary's to themes common to Dorothea's story and Lydgate's—in other words, a change in the central issue of the novel from the course of childhood loves to the course of adult, of symbolic, aspirations. Thus the theme of a disjunction between a childhood in nature and visionary power in adulthood is reflected in the history of the novel's composition, indeed in the final slight disjunctiveness of the form of the novel. Both Dorothea and Lydgate aspire to an ideal synthesis of theory and practice. Dorothea yearns for "some lofty conception of the world which might frankly include the parish of Tipton and her own rule of conduct there" (chap. 1), and as his name Tertius (revised from the more romantic Tristram, a name more suitable to the original conception of the book) suggests, Lydgate's identity is to be the synthesis of a dialectic between a local medical practice and theoretic and scientific research. Aiming too high, too egotistically, without thought for limiting circumstances, both Dorothea and Lydgate have their aspirations revised downward for them, whether happily or not.

Mary and Fred's romance is successful because (after Fred recovers from his disinheritance) they have such moderate aspirations. The aspiration plot circulates around and beyond them, making their situation a comic version of the more profound difficulties experienced by Lydgate and Dorothea. The separation between their story and the two major stories is Eliot's vision of Wordsworth writ large. What Fred and Mary succeed at—the sustaining of a childhood love—seals them off from what most concern Dorothea and Lydgate, the search for a life adequate to the highest of imaginative needs. As in *The Mill on the Floss*, a childhood that resembles Wordsworth childhood but that is actually spent in loving someone else leads, not toward sublimity, but toward practical compromises in which larger possibilities for individual growth yield to loyalty to the good of others.

Mary's love for Fred, never really questioned, is at one point defined against higher possibilities consciously and willingly foregone. Having understood in chapter 57 that Farebrother loves her,

> It was impossible to help fleeting visions of another kind—
> new dignities and an acknowledged value of which she had
> often felt the absence. But these things with Fred outside

them, Fred forsaken and looking sad for the want of her, could never tempt her deliberate thought.

Worded as a restriction, not just of possibility, but of thought itself, this passage follows a restatement of the importance of loyalty to ties formed in childhood:

> Mary earnestly desired to be always clear that she loved Fred best. When a tender affection has been storing itself in us through many of our years, the idea that we could accept any exchange for it seems to be a cheapening of our lives. And we can set a watch over our affections and our constancy as we can over other treasures.

Sympathetic as this passage is, its economic metaphor lends a chilling tone to its endorsement of what amounts to an illusion, even if it is a necessary and a beautiful illusion. Mary repeats this negative reasoning in defending her choice to her father in the last chapter. After saying that she loved Fred "because I have always loved him," her half-joking tone shifts to seriousness: "I don't think either of us could spare the other, or like any one else better, however much we might admire them. It would make too great a difference to us—like seeing all the old places altered, and changing the name for everything."

Such a love is a defense against the fragility of identity and the arbitrariness of language. It provides a clue to life, but it is a choice of feeling that excludes thought. Many readers have found it difficult to share Eliot's interest in and sympathy for Fred, but Fred's value in the story is his lack of admirable qualities. Through him Eliot can test the power of loyalty to childhood loves, without which he would be quite far from what Mary—consulting other faculties besides her loyalty—might wish for in a husband. The entertaining of "fleeting visions of another kind" would shake the very basis of identity, and this love, the getting and providing of security, is a defense against the effects of such visions. Like Maggie and the sonnets' little sister, Mary seeks a secure identity at the price of possibility; she cannot have both (as Wordsworth can). The difference is that while Maggie minds terribly, Mary minds hardly at all; marrying Farebrother would hardly have been for her an experience of the sublime. Still, the danger to her identity threatened by her "fleeting visions" recalls the difference between Wordsworth's experience of imaginative vision as a child and that of Maggie or of the little sister in the sonnet sequence. While for Wordsworth vision leads to further visions, Eliot's heroines must refuse vision in favor of, or convert it by literalizing it into, the machinery of a more prosaic life. That Mary thrives happily on this literalization, while Maggie does not, suggests Eliot's effort to make the impossibility for women of Wordsworthian vision seem as advantageous for her heroines as it is for her own writing. Labeling with Wordworth's terms for his own childhood the portrayal of a childhood that leads to a happily un–Wordsworthian adult life. Eliot obtains Wordsworth's authority for severing the poet's own connection between childhood in nature and the growth of visionary imagination.

At the very start of the novel, as Eliot finally assembled and rewrote it, Dorothea's plot of revised aspirations begins with a scene involving her mother, a mother whose distant but distinct resemblance to Maggie's mother suggests that, like Mary's, Dorothea's turn away from visionary possibility will resemble, though far less disastrously, Maggie's literalizing life. Much as Mrs. Tulliver's life is wholly absorbed in inert things, all we know of Dorothea's mother is her association with objects and their capacity for distracting women's attention from more visionary or "theoretic" aims. Maggie's mother is alive and therefore not available to the kind of figurative replacement to which Wordsworth's mother yields, but even though Dorothea's mother is dead, her meaning for her daughter is much closer to that of Maggie's mother than of Wordsworth's. In the first scene of the novel, Dorothea and Celia are discussing the division of their mother's silent legacy of jewels in a way that emblematizes the general shift Dorothea makes over the course of the novel from yearning toward theory to accepting available actuality. The sisters' values at first seem polarized: Celia loves jewels and especially her appearance in them, while Dorothea in the light of her religious theories considers them vanities. But when by coincidence "the sun passing beyond a cloud sent a bright gleam over the table," which forces her to see "how very beautiful these gems are" (chap. 1), Dorothea's clear spiritual vision becomes confused, and the scene ends in Celia's concluding that her sister is "not always consistent." Dorothea's confusion results from an accidental resemblance between the worst of female vanity and the highest spiritual value, a resemblance that obliges her to try "to justify her delight in the colours by merging them in her mystic religious joy." Like the accidents of Maggie and the little sister catching fish while doing what is considered wrong, the coincidence here of spiritual and literal is the start of Dorothea's long learning that her "theoretic" mind must bend to circumstances and to the senses, her individual vision to social practice.

That the jewels are all that remain of Dorothea's mother, and that the worldly Celia (who later styles herself as matron) inherits almost all of them, establishes a connection between the dead mother and the world of objects, senses, and circumstances that initially opposes Dorothea's ardent theorizing. Mrs. Brooke's jewels are only a more tasteful version of Mrs. Tulliver's ugly hats, spotted table linens, tippets, and frills. Dorothea's failure to make a convincing coherence between her sensual response to her mother's jewels and her theory about them repeats our sense about Maggie that for a woman there is no "mother tongue of the imagination" (*Mill on the Floss,* bk. 1, chap. 5). Unlike the mother Wordsworth reinvents in the form of nature, these heroines' mothers endorse limitation and literal repetition. Where theory and an actual good do not coincide, Dorothea learns to prefer actuality, and this choice is defined as female.

Dorothea's resemblance to Maggie in this scene is carried out in various ways in the rest of the novel. It is clear from the start that Dorothea will find no path, clear or circuitious, from adolescent ardor to a life that will satisfy the demands of theory. In this book "written for grown-up people," there is no fishing scene, but when Dorothea is "sobbing bitterly" to herself in Rome, in chapter 20, she is at the same turning point where we have seen Maggie and the sonnets' little sister, where what might have been a road to the sublime is barred by the pressure of other needs. (The situation also resembles Cathy's turning back to childhood in *Wuthering Heights,* whereas her author, as well as Jane Eyre and her author, adopt symbolic ways.) She is in the process of realizing that she has married the wrong man—an utterly innocent error, like Maggie's and the little sister's, yet with far greater practical consequences even than Wordsworth's transgression in stealing the rowboat. She experiences about her marriage a "feeling of desolation" that is heightened by the "stupendous fragmentariness" of Rome with its "gigantic broken revelations," its "ruins and basilicas, palaces and colossi," its "vast wreck of ambitious ideals, sensuous and spiritual." In her innocence and simplicity of heart, she has "no . . . defence against deep impressions," and the epigraph confirms that she is at this point a vulnerable child:

> A child foresaken, waking suddenly,
> Whose gaze afeard on all things round doth rove,
> And seeth only that it cannot see
> The meeting eyes of love.

This scene of a bewildered child whose mind, caught at a moment of moral crisis, is battered by gigantic broken revelations, recalls the way in which Maggie and the little sister of the sonnets revise the child's experience in the boat-stealing scene in *The Prelude*. Just as Wordsworth's vision is blocked by "solitude / Or blank desertion" and turned inward so that he cannot see "familiar shapes" or the "colours of green fields," Dorothea's desolation turns her vision inward so that she blames herself for her marriage and internalizes the vast awfulness of Rome. The "huge and mighty forms" Wordsworth inwardly sees instead are his intimation of the imaginative vision into which he is growing. Wordsworth characteristically figures such visitations in just this way, as the replacement, often very abrupt, of an outer light by an inner one. In the Intimations Ode, the poet is grateful for "Those shadowy recollections, / Which . . . Are yet a master light of all our seeing"; or in the Simplon Pass passage from *The Prelude*, "the light of sense / Goes out, but with a flash that has revealed / The invisible world" (bk. 6, ll. 600–602).

For Dorothea, however, the replacement of outer by inner light produces effects opposite to those that occur in Wordsworth. When Will sees her in the Vatican in chapter 19, she seems to be gazing, not at the statues, but at a streak of sunlight on the floor. But after the narrator's long discussion of Rome and marriage we learn that

> she did not really see the streak of sunlight on the floor more than she saw the statues: she was inwardly seeing the light of years to come in her own home and over the English fields and elms and hedge-bordered highroads; and feeling that the way in which they might be filled with joyful devotedness was not so clear to her as it had been.
>
> (chap. 20)

When Dorothea is, like Wordsworth at his highest moments in inward vision, blind to sunlight and to statues, her inner seeing of an inner light reveals to her ironically only the grimmest of realistic pictures. "The light of years to come" represents a light that is closer to the common day into which the clouds of glory in the Intimations Ode fade than it is to the "master light" of visionary seeing. Where Wordsworth's blank desertion supervises the conversion of an actual "huge peak" into "huge and mighty forms" within the mind, Dorothea's desolation signals no creative power. It is that inward vision itself, and its inevitable fulfillment, against which she is in most need of defenses.

It is at the moment of her turning away from romantic vision— which is in any case, not visionary, but a realistic envisioning—that Will visits her, and his visit seals her choice by providing something toward which to turn. What she turns toward in Will is, as is true also for Mary and for Maggie, an imagined past. The narrator says of the change in Dorothea's perception of her marriage that "the light had changed, and you cannot find the pearly dawn at noonday" (chap. 20). Yet the pearly dawn is just what Will offers her: a reversion to innocence and to a metaphoric childhood to accompany her turning away from the desolateness of private consciousness and visionary power. Will and Dorothea are consistently described as children when together or thinking of each other, so that figuratively they become a childhood couple much like Maggie and Tom or Mary and Fred. Each seems younger than the other at their first meeting in Rome. Coming out of her room to greet him,

> there were just signs enough that she had been crying to make her open face look more youthful and appealing than usual. . . . He was the elder by several years, but at that moment he looked much the younger, for his transparent complexion flushed suddenly.
>
> (chap. 21)

Later, Will grants himself and Dorothea an Edenic past before the catastrophic misunderstanding occasioned when Dorothea sees him with Rosamond:

> Until that wretched yesterday . . . all their vision, all their thought of each other, had been as in a world apart, where the sunshine fell on tall white lilies, where no evil lurked, and no other soul entered. But now—would Dorothea meet him in that world again?
>
> (chap. 82)

This prelinguistic, Edenic past of perfect mutual understanding is of course completely illusory. But, like the narrator's assertion in *The Mill on the Floss* that Maggie and Tom have had an Edenic childhood, and like the disjunctive description of childhood's beloved landscape in relation to the rest of the novel—their belief in it is what secures the permanence of their love. If Dorothea is the child in the epigraph, waking afraid, she turns from desolate absence to "the meeting eyes of love" of Will, who offers through a return to an imaginary childhood a way out of the impasse into which her vision leads.

In the larger program of the novel, Dorothea's choice of Will represents her final abandonment of her quest for a life of theory, a life as a subject within the symbolic order. Like Maggie's bliss at the round pool with Tom, Dorothea's and Will's vision of the past—their illusion of a shared childhood—demands fulfillment in terms of literal repetition, not of growth or change. Will's way of thinking about recovering Dorothea's love is "But now—would Dorothea meet him in that world again?" In offering a return to the "pearly dawn," Will offers Dorothea an improvement over Casaubon, but a light no more visionary than Casaubon's disappointing noon. She will replace the grim "light of years to come" with the light of hours or years gone by. This loving repetition of an imagined past excludes, with Dorothea's consent, what might remain of her individual vision and aspiration: "'It is quite true that I might be a wiser person, Celia,' said Dorothea, 'and that I might have done something better, if I had been better. But this is what I am going to do'" (chap. 84). For Dorothea, the realm of imaginative vision is always finally what might have been but will never be, not, as for Wordsworth, "something evermore about to be." Where flashes of inward light shift Wordsworth's narrative to a new level and lead to the poet's growth, the lights that Dorothea lives in are all ultimately variants on the light of day, and there is no visionary light that shines inwardly in contrast to an outer darkness or blindness. In Wordsworth, the hope that "Paradise, and groves / Elysian" will become "A simple produce of the common day" remains in the realm of prophecy; for Eliot's heroines, who ultimately dwell only in the light of prophecy; for Eliot's heroines, who ultimately dwell only in the light of common day, paradise remains retrospective, at best a saving illusion about the past.

One final light flashes before the close of Dorothea's story, in the scene in which Dorothea and Will finally agree to marry.

> There came a vivid flash of lightning which lit each of them up for the other—and the light seemed to be the terror of a hopeless love. Dorothea darted instantaneously from the window; Will followed her, seizing her hand with a spasmodic movement; and so they stood, with their hands clasped, like two children, looking out on the storm.
>
> (chap. 83)

The brief scene recapitulates the salient features of the scene in Rome. Light that seems to be interior usurps the place of inward light and illuminates a relationship instead of an individual consciousness. Although the feelings involved are entirely opposite, "the light of years to come in her own home," which is after all not her own home but Casaubon's, is not far in kind from this light "which lit each of them up for the other." This seeing in which vision that seems interior is of the other, not of the self, is followed in both cases with a turn toward Will and toward a figurative childhood: "like two children."

The only imaginable happy end for Dorothea, by this point, is the literalization, or literal reproduction, of that figurative childhood. In marrying Will, Dorothea may give up her quest for a life of theory, "feeling that there was always something better which she might have done," but the "small row of cousins at Freshitt who enjoyed playing with the two cousins visiting Timpton" literalize and so confirm the happy childhood in the Midlands landscape that has been only figurative for their parents. Dorothea's abandonment of the "something better" she might have done resembles Mary's cleaving to Fred by keeping herself from thinking of "fleeting visions," and likewise Dorothea's final literalization of a figurative childhood resembles Mary's future, which consists of its happy repetition of the past. Turning from "possibility" back to the solid reality of her childhood, Mary marries a man who will learn her father's trade and become almost as much a realist as he. Mary and Fred's last scene in the story guarantees this reproduction of the past, through their repetition of each other's words and through their recurrence to the original childhood action that has secured their love. Mary has just told Fred the news that he is to live in Stone Court and earn its possession:

> "Pray don't joke, Mary," said Fred, with strong feeling. "Tell me seriously that all this is true, and that you are happy because of it—because you love me best."
>
> "It is all true, Fred, and I am happy because of it—because I love you best," said Mary, in a tone of obedient recitation.
>
> They lingered on the door-step under the steep-roofed porch, and Fred almost in a whisper said—
>
> "When we were first engaged, with the umbrella ring, Mary, you used to—"
>
> The spirit of joy began to laugh more decidedly in Mary's eyes.
>
> (chap. 86)

And the future sketched in the finale is an entirely happy repetition of the past:

> On inquiry it might possibly be found that Fred and Mary still inhabit Stone Court . . . that on sunny days the two lovers

who were first engaged with the umbrella-ring may be seen in white-haired placidity at the open window from which Mary Garth, in the days of old Peter Featherstone, had often been ordered to look out for Mr. Lydgate.

While Maggie's docilely female repetitions kill her, Mary's bring happiness. Likewise, Mary's relation as a reader and writer to prior texts is a comic version of Maggie's. Mary's "Stories of Great Men, taken from Plutarch," transformations of formal, abstract Latin prose into English and presumably into her lively narrative style, is the literary counterpart of her other docile female repetitions. That its authorship is attributed to Fred, the former classical scholar, reinforces the containment of this writing within Victorian paradigms of female propriety. At the same time, the title, "taken from Plutarch," suggests a daring theft, undertaken under the cover of such propriety. This comically ambiguous situation recalls that of Mary Ann in the sonnet about Scott, in which it is unclear whether "wrote the tale" means authoritative and prior invention or daughterly veneration; and it is the sonnet's ambiguity as to deference or originality that models Eliot's own practice with respect to Wordsworth.

If Mary's fate is a comic version of Maggie's, Dorothea's likewise a happier version of the abandonment of theory or vision for the literal. And yet that Dorothea nearly dies in giving birth to the first of the "small row of cousins," to the literal embodiment of her figurative past, recalls the danger associated with childbirth's reproduction of the self as child in the Brontës' novels. The danger of the literal of which Maggie dies is echoed when Celia, anticipating the news of Dorothea's marriage, thinks "of her sister as the dangerous part of the family machinery" (chap. 84). The dark overtones of the finale's closing account of Dorothea allude particularly to Maggie's fate: the characterization of "her full nature" as a river that "spent itself in channels which had no great name on the earth" recalls the river in which Maggie drowns; and that those like Dorothea "rest in unvisited tombs," in the closing words of the novel, recalls the tomb of Maggie and Tom, visited by Philip, Stephen, and Lucy. If Mary Garth and the little girl writing Scott's novel in the sonnet offer enactments of Eliot's own myth of female literary transmission—apparently submissive, yet changing the ending—enactments that suggest Eliot's contentment with that myth, the Maggie-tints in Dorothea suggest otherwise, that the inevitability of women's variance from the Wordworthian model brings, not only power, but also pain.

"The Dark Woman Triumphs": Passion in *The Mill on the Floss*

Gillian Beer

The Mill on the Floss first raises in an acute form the besetting problem to which George Eliot constantly returns. Is the only form of heroism open to women to be martyrdom? And should women accept that form of heroism at all? Heroism in literature is represented in many forms for men, martyrdom among them. But for women martyrdom has been the most powerful single channel for narrative activity and narrative conclusion. In *Clarissa* we have the most extensive form of the paradox. Clarissa's sensibility is accorded an extraordinary range and complexity. Her values impress the values of the narrative. The text is "lisible" only by means of an accord between reader and the figure of Clarissa. Despite our frequent treacherous complicity with Lovelace, our pleasure in his insights and stratagems, our reading can find repose only by recourse to the writing of Clarissa, whose own discourse is whole, not fractured, not polymorphic, though constantly opposed and interrupted by the events and counter-events of other people's letters.

It is this wholeness, this integrity, which conducts her towards martyrdom. Lovelace never makes choices; he doubles them. When she makes choices, she renounces other possibilities. So the text, as labyrinth, apes the form of Lovelace; the text as consequential sequence requires the presence—and the sacrifice—of Clarissa. As the book proceeds, more and more choices are fictitiously presented to her by the activities of Lovelace. These dream-choices, fictive possibilities, brush past her without impinging on her real situation, which is that of enclosure, resistance

From *George Eliot* (Key Women Writers Series), edited by Sue Rose. © 1986 by Gillian Beer. Harvester, 1986.

and isolation. She attempts escape and is brought back. She is surrounded by the treachery of other women. Even Anna Howe for a time misunderstands and abandons her. She is raped. She survives. "Clarissa lives." Her integrity, it proves, does not only rely upon her physical intactness. And yet she is elected to die. One by one the choices are closed down around her. She does not marry Lovelace. She does not retire to the country to manage in independence the estate left to her by her grandfather, a solution which Victorian women writers came to favour, as we have seen. Instead she organises her own death, writing her letters upon her coffin, in an epigrammatic domestication of her dilemma and her solution. She will claim death. Or Richardson will claim it for her.

Many of his women correspondents protested against the process of foreclosing which they saw happening. They tried to save her from his sacrificial act. He used his authority as author, originator, patriarch, to bring her—with infinite compunction—to death. Was he offering a critique of the current social order which made no space for women like Clarissa? Was he saving her for himself? Was he claiming for her the only form of epic action open to women—a sacrificial epic in which the woman, like Lucrece, sustains her integrity by self-immolation? He divests Clarissa's death of all suggestion of punishment. It is a Christ-like sacrifice, but, unlike Christ, it does not redeem. It demonstrates.

Perhaps it is worth noting that George Eliot seems to have appreciated *Sir Charles Grandison* more than *Clarissa,* and found its women's witty capacity for survival more pleasurable than Clarissa's long renunciation and assertion of the will. But that does not at all mean that she was less affected by *Clarissa.* . . . She resists its allurements precisely because they are so alluring to her. Of her heroines, only one, Maggie, shares Clarissa's fate—and then in the tumult of accident rather than as sustained choice. So Maggie may have her release and her fulfilment without being implicated in the will to death. That is not to say, however, that she is exempted from the will to martyrdom.

George Eliot found it necessary to distinguish between renunciation and martyrdom. Her men are inclined to accuse women of a will to martyrdom when what they are observing is a will to independence. In a social order which constrains women, of course, the desire for independence and for martyrdom may prove to have indistinguishable consequences, but they are not indistinguishable in their natures. The reality of choice is crucial in George Eliot's work. People frequently make choices before they have observed it (as Lydgate does in his impulse to comfort

Rosamond which results in his engagement). But they recognise choice, even if retrospectively. What are the areas of choice open to women?

In a long review of George Eliot's career up to 1863, Richard Simpson argues that

> The antithesis of passion and duty figures itself to her mind as a kind of sexual distinction; so that if woman could be defecated from all male fibres, she would be all passion, as man, purged of all feminine qualities, would be all hard duty.

He then neatly turns the screw of this argument a round further:

> It is natural that the authoress should make her women act male parts, and give her men something of a feminine character. Though she ought to be able to draw woman in herself, for the simple reason that she is a woman, yet she may be too far separated from the ordinary life of her sex to be a good judge of its relations. The direct power and the celebrity of authorship may obscure and replace the indirect influence and calm happiness of domestic feminine life. . . . Having thus taken up the male position, the male ideal becomes hers,—the ideal of power,—which, interpreted by her feminine heart and intellect, means the supremacy of passion in the affairs of the world.

Simpson shares the wearisome assumption that men can naturally portray women but not women men. However, the fear that she might have separated herself too far from the ordinary is one which George Eliot saw as the special difficulty of the woman artist, as we shall see in "Armgart," and again in *Daniel Deronda*. Simpson here contrives to blame her both for being tainted with masculinity and femininity. Nevertheless, the point he makes about the *power* of the author is not one to be passed over lightly. By claiming "the male position" (what he elsewhere calls "direct power through reasoning and speech") she has, according to his analysis, forfeited contact with the actual social condition of women. "She gives us her view of woman's vocation, and paints things as they ought to be, not as they are." Such criticism may help to account for the greater emphasis on typicality in the ordering of women in her late novels. No one after Maggie is allowed to issue out of her condition.

Many Victorian commentators characterised George Eliot as a novelist preoccupied with passion. If we identify passion solely with sexual love between peers we shall find a dearth of any extended description of such love-sensation in her work. Henry James commented on the singular austerity with which George Eliot treated love, suggesting that *Middlemarch* and *Daniel Deronda* did

> seem to foreign readers, probably, like vast, cold, commodious, respectable rooms, through whose window-panes one sees a snow-covered landscape, and across whose acres of sober-hued carpet one looks in vain for a fireplace or a fire.

It is necessary to insist, in our culture, that passion does not describe solely heterosexual love-affairs. If her representations of sexual encounter are at the opposite extreme of reticence from *My Secret Life*, it is worth remembering Foucault's comment that that work is part of the Victorian process of transforming sex into discourse. But if we understand passion in relationships as vehement human need sustained past the accomplishment of moments of desire, we shall more exactly mark what it meant for her.

A French critic in the 1870s, remarked that her writing was "très éloquent dans la peinture du remords, beaucoup moins animé pourtant quand il s'agit d'exprimer l'amour." This pinpoints exactly one of the human passions that she most fully understood: the obsessional reliving of the spent moment in an attempt to make it change its shape, to escape its shame and regret. Remorse is one of the most engrossing emotions for narrative, since it strives to recuperate a bearable reading, its obsessional repetition seeking to be rid of the need yet again to retell the same fixed story. George Eliot was able both through the organisation of repetition and through the analysis of its glaring fixity of recall to explore the passionate experience of remorse. Indeed, in *Daniel Deronda,* Gwendolen's self-discovery is fuelled almost entirely by remorse.

In Maggie, passion takes the form of vehement intellectual need experienced as emotion. Desire for knowledge, for "more instruments playing together," had traditionally been enregistered as the man's story. Faust and his wild passion for full possession of the world that knowledge may open, is saved by the innocent, stay-at-home, untutored Gretchen. Steadfast love is divided from the thirst for knowledge, polarised as female and male. George Eliot rejects that polarisation, first in Maggie, and then, more and more powerfully in the later novels by means of the polymathic narrative which, through learning, constantly discovers emotional connection. The writing ranges freely through and beyond such oppositions, but it also experiences them. In "Armgart" we are presented with the urgency of creative anger and need—an anger which is generated more by desire than by frustration, and a desire which is for the creative act itself:

> I carry my revenges in my throat;
> I love in singing, and am loved again.

Several feminist critics, notably Christ (1976) and Midler (1980), have pointed out the urgency of anger in George Eliot's creativity and her need, also, to reach beyond anger. In her anger, although there is often an edge of frustration and criticism of current social forms, there is frequently also a more Pythian "rage." Not all anger is social reformist nor seeking solution.

Charlotte Brontë shows the same phenomenon in a more pronounced form. Contemporary critics were to some extent at a loss to describe what they found so disturbing in her work. The *Blackwood's* reviewer set it alongside seditious acts and European revolt. The surging vehemence of *claim* subverted steady forms. And we find this claim in the activity of telling, as well as in what is told. Writing, making, publishing, are all claims to space and attention. The form of first person in *Jane Eyre,* and the centrality of Maggie's intellectual growth in *The Mill,* assert the importance of unregarded life. They make us *recognise* that life. George Eliot's special attention is given to "unhistoric acts" and to individual lives without national importance. She shows such lives and such acts as being embroiled in movements recognisable from history books. She raises the unregarded into significance. Her use of double time-schemes in all her works except *Daniel Deronda* means that the reader is required not only to recognise the past but to appraise the present in a carefully experimental series of relations to the past.

Elaine Showalter (1977) sees the story of Maggie Tulliver as George Eliot's concession to a particularly Victorian configuration of the female which produces a "passive, self-destructive heroine." This reading makes Maggie sound more renunciatory than she is portrayed as being in the book. As Nina Auerbach (1982) shows, Maggie is connected from the beginning of the story with the demonic.

> "Oh I'll tell you what that means. It's a dreadful picture, isn't it? But I can't help looking at it. That old woman in the water's a witch—they've put her in to find out whether she's a witch or no, and if she swims she's a witch, if she's drowned—and killed, you know—she's innocent, and not a witch, but only

a poor silly old woman. But what good would it do her then, you know, when she was drowned? Only, I suppose, she'd go to heaven, and God would make it up to her."

(bk. 1, chap. 3)

Maggie here cites the tale of the witch in Defoe's *History of the Devil*. The witch epitomises Maggie's bind. If she is innocent, she drowns. If she bobs up again, she is guilty. Is Maggie's drowning used in some half-magical way to prove her innocence? If so, such innocence is useless. Like the witch, Maggie is dead. Only the narrator can "make it up to her." The last chapter, indeed, is entitled "The Final Rescue," and that rescue is undertaken by the writer. Within the work, Maggie herself makes jokes about another such magical ordering in novels and fairy tales, that of the blond and the dark heroine. The blond represents restraint and social order, the dark, passion and disruption. The blond is bound to win, and Maggie resents that. So do we. Lucy sees Maggie's learning as "witchcraft": "part of your general uncanniness" (bk. 6, chap. 3).

> "I didn't finish the book," said Maggie. "As soon as I came to the blond-haired young lady reading in the park, I shut it up, and determined to read no further. I foresaw that that light-complexioned girl would win away all the love from Corinne and make her miserable. I'm determined to read no more books where the blond-haired women carry away all the happiness. I should begin to have a prejudice against them. If you could give me some story, now, where the dark woman triumphs, it would restore the balance. I want to avenge Rebecca and Flora MacIvor, and Minna and all the rest of the dark unhappy ones."
>
> (bk. 5, chap. 4)

The work playfully draws attention to its own order and knowingly prognosticates what comes to seem inevitable: Maggie's defeat. Yet it presages, too, the paradoxical sense of Maggie's triumph and vengeance with which, despite her death, the book concludes.

The novel is full of meaning glimpsed from earlier literature. Maggie is determinedly shut out by the education system, with its stereotypes of male and female, from classical learning, though she demonstrates her readiness and skill at Mr Stelling's house. But the magical fragmentariness also feeds her:

> She presently made up her mind to skip the rules in the Syn-

tax—the examples became so absorbing. The mysterious sentences, snatched from an unknown context,—like strange horns of beasts, and leaves of unknown plants, brought from some far-off region—gave boundless scope to her imagination, and were all the more fascinating because they were in a peculiar tongue of their own, which she could learn to interpret.

(bk. 2, chap. 1)

Both Tom and Maggie, for differing reasons, are dependent on Philip, the wounded Philoctetes, to give them access to the warmth of learning in their lives. The roused meaning of flat text needs a speaking voice to make it heard. Learning can enter their youth as story:

He listened with great interest to a new story of Philip's about a man who had a very bad wound in his foot, and cried out so dreadfully with the pain that his friends could bear with him no longer, but put him ashore on a desert island, with nothing but some wonderful poisoned arrows to kill animals with for food.

"I didn't roar out a bit, you know," Tom said, "and I daresay my foot was as bad as his. It's cowardly to roar."

But Maggie would have it that when anything hurt you very much, it was quite permissible to cry out, and it was cruel of people not to bear it. She wanted to know if Philoctetes had a sister, and why *she* didn't go with him on the desert island and take care of him.

(bk. 2, chap. 6)

These stories are shared complicitly by author and reader, weaving connections not always apparent to those within the text. Like metaphor, they allow meaning to emerge without settling. And yet George Eliot will not allow the reader to remain comfortable within the possession of these connections: "light irony" and easy cultural pretensions may be bought dear, and Maggie's "false quantities" go with a deeper learning than Tom's.

Now and then, that sort of enthusiasm finds a far-echoing voice that comes from an experience springing out of the deepest need. And it was by being brought within the long lingering vibrations of such a voice that Maggie, with her girl's face and unnoted sorrows, found an effort and a hope that helped her through years of loneliness, making out a faith for herself without the aid of established authorities and appointed guides—for they were not at hand, and her need was pressing.

(bk. 4, chap. 3)

Thomas à Kempis's *Imitation of Christ* speaks to Maggie as voice, in a way that is made to sustain the emphasis of the address to the reader immediately afterwards.

But good society, floated on gossamer wings of light irony, is of very expensive production; requiring nothing less than a wide and arduous national life condensed in unfragrant deafening factories, cramping itself in mines, sweating at furnaces, grinding, hammering, weaving under more or less oppression of carbonic acid—or else, spread over sheep-walks, and scattered in lonely houses and huts on the clayey or chalky cornlands, where the rainy days look dreary. This wide national life is based entirely on emphasis—the emphasis of want.

Philip says of himself "'my voice is middling—like everything else in me.'" But Philip is the interpreter, a redeemed version of Latimer, able despite his physical debility to see precisely and kindly into the sensibility of others. He is kind, in some ways more kind or "kinned" to Maggie than her brother, though in the end it is blood-bond and primitive memory that hold her. His exclusion from active life sets him alongside Maggie in a way which confuses likeness and difference. He tempts Maggie with his offer to be "brother and teacher," but he can never satisfy her sexually.

For Maggie, there can be no accommodation with society, because the community in which she has grown up, and the culture of which this is an expression, will accord her nature no recognition.

"Girls can't do Euclid: can they, sir?"

"They can pick up a little of everything, I daresay," said Mr Stelling. "They've a great deal of superficial cleverness; but they couldn't go far into anything. They're quick and shallow." . . . As for Maggie, she had hardly ever been so mortified. She had been so proud to be called "quick" all her little life, and now it appeared that this quickness was the brand of inferiority.

(bk. 2, chap. 1)

She is one of the aberrations of breeding:

> "An' a pleasant sort o' soft woman may go on breeding you
> stupid lads and cute wenches, till it's like as if the world was
> turned topsy-turvey."
>
> > (bk. 1, chap. 3)

She resists bonding herself to other women, because they represent so
much she must gainsay.

> "I think all women are crosser than men," said Maggie.
> "Aunt Glegg's a great deal crosser than Uncle Glegg, and
> mother scolds me more than father does."
>
> "Well, *you'll* be a woman some day," said Tom, "so *you*
> needn't talk."
>
> "But I shall be a *clever* woman," said Maggie, with a toss.
>
> "Oh, I daresay, and a nasty conceited thing. Everybody'll
> hate you."
>
> > (bk. 2, chap. 1)

The work excels at taut humour which catches the sound of women
gossiping, pinched into the forms of their narrow society. The aunts with
cheerful gloom give voice to the domestic powers and repression of St
Ogg's.

Maggie's other favourite childhood reading, *Pilgrim's Progress,* is a
story of tribulations ending in triumph and delight. Loved as that model
is, it is also eschewed, though something of its mood of triumphal rec-
oncilement is retained. Like Christian, Maggie and Tom go down into
the river. Through careful, humanistic negatives, George Eliot allows a
secular faith in human accord to predict this final scene:

> There was an undefined sense of reconcilement with her
> brother: what quarrel, what harshness, what unbelief in each
> other can subsist in the presence of a great calamity, when all
> the artificial vesture of our life is gone, and we are all one
> with another in primitive mortal needs?
>
> > (bk. 7, chap. 5)

The book refuses to consider the question: how long can that oneness
survive after calamity?—unless Tom and Maggie's immediate death implies a dour answer.

The brother-sister relationship had a particular significance for
George Eliot. There were literary-historical as well as biographical reasons for its power. She came a generation after the romantic writers, and

in particular her much reverenced Wordsworth, had made of the relationship an epipsychidion: a marriage of the soul with itself, the yolk and white of Plato's parable. George Eliot's intense childhood relationship with her brother, always perhaps more intense on her side than his, and their complete rupture after she went to live with Lewes, form a complete and punctuated story on which, painfully, she continued to look back.

In narrative terms, the *containment* of the relationship within the period of her youth intensified its meaning. The identification of brother and sister and their subsequent rupture, created powerful metaphors for the growth of identity, which, in a just pre-Freudian age, could provide a symbolic discourse capable of analysing the Deronda-Gwendolen relationship as much as the Tom-Maggie relationship.

Antigone, her significant heroine, who stood against the authority of state and king, indeflectable, endured all to give her brother proper burial. Foucault writes in *The History of Sexuality*, I,

> When a long while ago the West discovered love, it bestowed
> on it a value high enough to make death acceptable; nowadays
> it is sex that claims this equivalence, the highest of all, . . .
> the fictitious point of sex . . . exerts enough charm on everyone
> for them to accept hearing the grumble of death within it.

In the story of Antigone, love, duty, kinship, passion and death grumble within one another. Sex is, in one sense, excluded. Yet through Antigone's passional commitment, erotic emotion permeates the story. Perhaps, too, we should pay attention to her desired act: to give her brother proper burial, to lay him to rest. To honour him and to be free of him. In the Antigone story, the consequence is that the heroine is buried alive. Maggie Tulliver drowns alongside Tom. But George Eliot survived after Marian Evans's alienation from her brother—was even born out of that alienation.

II

It would not suffice to provide a critique of *The Mill* in terms of the social realism that its conclusion outfaces. The opening equally with the ending disturbs sociological description. The book is enclosed within a preliminary dream, in which an unsexed narrator gradually converts a present so immediate that it seems at first to lack even verb, back into a warmed but vitiated past. The book opens with this sentence:

A wide plain, where the broadening Floss hurries on between

> its green banks to the sea, and the loving tide, rushing to meet
> it, checks its passage with an impetuous embrace.

The passional sweep, the lack of preliminaries, makes for an effusiveness
in that first description which is both embarrassing and opening. The
reader resists, and is swept along, is met by the verb "checks," whose
sense gives way into impetuous embrace. What is described is dilemma:
the downward hurrying river met by the in-rushing tide: the moment of
arrest and embrace is emphasised, just before permeation. We do not
know, since this is the opening, at what scope to read. We slide between
scales. Then, the eroticism of the opening sentence is yoked back into
economic order,

> the black ships—laden with the fresh-scented fir-planks, with
> rounded sacks of oil-bearing seed, or with the dark-glitter of
> coal—are borne along to the town of St Ogg's.

The senses (scent, touch, sight) are engaged and the second paragraph
ends with the description of the mill-stream:

> The stream is brimful now, and lies high in this withy plan-
> tation, and half drowns the grassy fringe of the croft. . . . As
> I look at the full stream, the vivid grass, the delicate bright-
> green powder softening the outline of the great trunks and
> branches that gleam from under the bare purple boughs, I am
> in love with moistness.

The knowledge of a seeing eye is brought close through touch: "I am in
love with moistness." The bodily intimacy of a fully-known landscape,
body-scape, is voiced in the first person. Plenitude is now. The writer
twice recurs to that metaphor of creative deafness which we have examined [elsewhere] in the tale of Parizade, once, in the quirky anthro-
pomorphism of the little river's "low placid voice, the voice of one who
is deaf and loving," and, again, in the mill-stream:

> The rush of the water, and the booming of the mill, bring a
> dreamy deafness, which seems to heighten the peacefulness of
> the scene. They are like a great curtain of sound, shutting one
> out from the world beyond.

Enclosure in another's dream—the creation of meta-memory—is the
project here. And that deep drop into irrecoverable intimacy preludes our
reading of the text. In "The Lifted Veil," written soon after beginning

The Mill, the entry into another's consciousness is combined with a recoil of memory which is threatening and arid. The first person here in *The Mill* is uncharacterised, and the end of the chapter has an awkward innocence of narrative technique about it, a plangent archness like that of Charles Lamb in "Dream Children." As so often with first person in George Eliot, the figure suggested is passive, here poised on the verge of maleness.

The opening, forgotten as we read on, has "left its trace, and lives in us still," though "blent irrecoverably" with later impressions in the text. The description of the river in the opening sentence is taken over into descriptions of Maggie's behaviour: "Maggie rushed to her deeds with passionate impulse" or

> For poor little Maggie had at once the timidity of an active imagination, and the daring that comes from overmastering impulse. She had rushed into the adventure of seeking her unknown kindred, the gypsies.
>
> (bk. 1, chap. 11)

At the end of the book the "dream-like" action of the flooded river reenters the narrative, taking with it Maggie who has lived alongside it, played by it and sometimes been identified with it. She has been threatened with drowning for her mischief with the water and has floated away with Stephen in the drift of need and desire. Finally, the two currents of river and tide meet and lock in the death-embrace of Tom and Maggie.

Perhaps it is exactly the assuaging of desire which is unsatisfying at the end. It is Maggie's flood, "uncannily" approaching to drown and rescue her. Throughout the book a sense of the "uncanniness" of inner life and the recalcitrance of outward circumstance have been equally maintained. In this book "tide" and "tidings," both insistent words, have kept each to its own domain of natural energy and narrative. But at the end they are confused.

Desire in this society cannot be satisfied. Maggie gives expression to desires which cannot be contained in any of the social forms available: "'I was never satisfied with a *little* of anything,'" she says to Philip, in renouncing him,

> "That is why it is better for me to do without earthly happiness altogether. . . . I never felt that I had enough music—I wanted more instruments playing together—I wanted voices to be fuller and deeper."
>
> (bk. 5, chap. 3)

It is this expression of female desire, the desire for knowledge, for sexual love, for free life, which is the unremitting narrative urgency of *The Mill on the Floss,* a desire for new forms of life unrealisable in terms of the old order and the fixed stereotypes by which she is surrounded. The desires (for knowledge, sexual love, freedom) are not different from those of men; the difference is in the breaking of the taboo on them, the claiming of them as female desires.

But the work is also combative towards its heroine. She is unremittingly tested, despite those guard words such as "poor Maggie," "poor child," which seem to offer her shelter. The intimacy and the unremittingness together create the particular tonic insight of the work; it becomes implacably opposed to half-measures. It is in these terms, also, that the ending is best understood. Maggie drowns. She sloughs off compromise. The narrative finally rejects the form of bildungsroman, in which the growing ego of a young man comes to terms with the society in which it dwells and accepts both attrition and continuity. Maggie's *bildung* takes her only to the point where she knows that there is no place for her in her own community, since she has rowed away with Stephen and returned not married to him. All would have been forgiven in time if they had married. But her individualistic insistence on old attachments, not on social forms, puts her irrevocably at odds with the codes by which her community is conditioned, despite their lip-service to kinship. In George Eliot's later books aggression, anger and frustration become more openly menacing energies, expressed in narrative as well as persons. In *The Mill on the Floss* Maggie's anger finds it very difficult to place itself without threatening her most deeply needed relationships (with Tom, with her father). So it recoils upon herself. She internalises it as self-doubt and inadequacy. Passionate feeling and passionate knowledge must both be *grown out of* if she is to survive in her environment.

Her swollen trouble, the outrage which cannot be countenanced as self-assertion, at the end of the book is naturalised as flood. In that way she cannot be held responsible for it. The sense of Maggie ceasing to be responsible, of her being freed from the inevitability of the social constraint and contract to which she has subdued herself, must trouble readers. Her heart's desire—the return to childhood, erotic reunion with her brother, the knitting up again of the divided self which has been split into the twin forms of male and female each with their separate order: these are desires which it is given to all to feel and none to fulfil. That is why she must die: she has refused Stephen *Guest,* the fleeting displacement of an older desire, as his name suggests.

The level of desire explored at the end of the book is *a-historical,* and ceases to be focused as a criticism of a specific social order. Up to that point, when it seemed that Maggie must endure attrition, misunderstanding, the drudging work of being a governess, the mode of the novel has been that of social critique: a recognition of the grinding power of social mores which are *capable of being changed.* Maggie's release removes the question of social change. Society's treatment of her is first brought into question, and then the question is set aside.

Floods may happen. The flooding river is part of the natural conditions which have produced the particular economic order of St. Ogg's. The flood thus has meanings which pull in opposing directions: outside the social and yet within economic order, there is always the possibility of uncontrollable natural event which comes willy-nilly and must take its course. At the same time, the analogy with sexual passion is strong, and particularly with female passion. Among the seventeenth-century musicians and lyricists whom Maggie admires such imagery is common:

> Weep, O mine eyes, and cease not:
> Your spring-tides, alas, methinks increase not,
> O when, O when begin you
> To swell so high that I may drown me in you?

So, as individual and as sexual symbol, the flood is Maggie's. "She was not bewildered for an instant—she knew it was the flood." The Floss has been persistently connected with the reawakening of her desire:

> And beyond, the silvery breadth of the dear old Floss . . . Maggie's eye began to fill with tears. . . . Memory and imagination urged upon her a sense of privation too keen to let her taste what was offered in the transient present: her future, she thought, was likely to be worse than her past, for after her years of contented renunciation, she had slipped back into desire and longing.
>
> (bk. 6, chap. 2)

But the Floss is also connected with memory as admonition: "If the past is not to bind us, where can duty lie?" She had floated downstream with Stephen. Now the flood removes the confines of stream: "There was no choice of courses, no room for hesitation, and she floated into the current." "Swiftly she went now, without effort" (bk. 7, chap. 5).

The freedom that Maggie is offered is the removal of choice. She had made the utmost effort of choice and of will in renouncing Stephen.

She had chosen martyrdom. Now choice is no longer demanded of her. She can float with the current. And the current restores her to "primitive mortal needs":

> the strong resurgent love towards her brother that swept away all the later impressions of hard, cruel offence and misunderstanding, and left only the deep, underlying, unshakeable memories of early union.
>
> (bk. 7, chap. 5)

a union which is realised in the death-embrace: "brother and sister had gone down in an embrace never to be parted."

This *liebestod,* the consummation of a union for which there is no place in the social order, is a deeper psychic challenge to the reader than the repudiated union with Stephen—a union which, through outside marriage, mimics parallel social forms. In the union of Maggie and Tom there is both the fullness of incestuous love, and a claim for a profound reconstitution of male and female. The knitting-up is an acceptance of male and female, which in education are estranged into socialised gender roles. Otto Rank suggests of the Oedipus myth that incest is a symbol of man's "self-creative urge." And here, lateral incest, the twinning and recombination of opposed selves, may be the expression of another "self-creative urge."

But it is an acceptance which can find its form and moment only in death. It is not envisaged as a part of life. It is summation, but it also expresses nostalgia for an earlier world here cleansed of its complexity. Within the novel we have *not* much seen Maggie and Tom in childhood with their little hands clasped in love, roaming the daisied fields together. There is only one episode where he is not cross or domineering towards her. We have seen them at odds, awkwardly fond, never finding quite how to fit together, tugging apart in their individual needs.

The end of the book sets up double-binds of the kind that Maggie had observed much earlier when in her early childhood she read Defoe's *History of the Devil* and embarrassed her father with her improper knowledge of the way the world treats women whom it selects as deviants. At the end of *The Mill on the Floss,* Maggie drowns, and is innocent, and receives her reward momentously and in an unsustainable instant in this world. She has rowed safely back to the mill. Tom, seeing the "huge fragments, clinging together in fatal fellowship" approaching them, reacts thus: "'It is coming, Maggie!' Tom said, in a deep hoarse voice, loosing the oars, and clasping her."

The orgasmic reference is overwhelming, and overwhelms them: and so does the flood. The transgressions that George Eliot liberates at the end of the novel are in that same moment suppressed and done away with. Opposing forces appear not in the calm of enigma but in the vehemence of conclusion. Conclusion permits events without consequences and without social force.

Lawrence ironises this episode in *Women in Love* by removing it from its privileged position as conclusion, and transferring blame to the female, turning it back into an image of the male entrapped. In George Eliot both man and woman are freed from that need to *blame* which, increasingly, she recognises in her writing and which the writing makes the reader recognise in herself and himself. But here she has not yet found a way of removing blame without removing consequences. By this I mean that the end of *The Mill on the Floss* cannot quite sustain both social enquiry and individual need.

Much later in her life, George Eliot, commenting on the social parallels between fiction and the conditions which produced her creative memories remarked to Emily Davies that things were worse in that society than she had shown them in the novel: "She considers that in *The Mill on the Floss,* everything is softened, as compared with real life. Her own experience she said was worse."

In the same conversation, using (if Emily Davies correctly recollects the metaphorical terms) images which draw on the terms of the novel, she said that her purpose in writing it

> was to show the conflict which is going on everywhere when
> the young generation with its higher culture comes into col-
> lision with the older, and in which, she said, so many young
> hearts make shipwreck far worse than Maggie.

That conversation took place while she was writing *Middlemarch,* which itself continues to examine the curtailing conditions which chafe the young into seeking freer forms for experience and activity. In *Middlemarch* there is no ready escape route, no naturalisation of thanatos as a feasible liberation from the demands of ordinary existence. The subversive vehemence of Maggie's fate both releases from the bounds of social realism and yet neutralises its own commentary by allowing her (and so us) the plenitude which is nowhere available within her society.

Ruskin, writing after George Eliot's death in 1881 fulminates against the ordinariness of the people in *The Mill* and sees them as valueless because typical:

> There is not a single person in the book of the smallest importance to anybody in the world but themselves, or whose qualities deserved so much as a line of printer's type in their description. There is no girl alive, fairly clever, half educated, and unluckily related, whose life has not at least as much in it as Maggie's, to be described and to be pitied . . . while the rest of the characters are simply the sweepings out of a Pentonville omnibus.

To George Eliot, they were valuable *because* typical, because they could stand for many others besides themselves. For other girls alive and other boys, whose situation is not usually described or pitied. Tom, as George Eliot insists, is as much a victim of rigid stereotyping as is Maggie. His schooling might have suited Maggie, frustrated with lack of learning, but stultifies Tom. On Tom falls the full weight of required manliness, sealing him into a pig-headed dutifulness and burdening him too young with certainty.

Richard Jenkyn comments on George Eliot's counter-creed to that of Greek tragedy: "The phrase *ti megethos* a "certain largeness" [which Maggie's small child action of pushing Lucy in the mud lacks] . . . is taken from Aristotle, who argued that the action of a tragedy had to have a certain greatness or grandeur to it. George Eliot rejects this view." But "a certain largeness" *is* required and created: the largeness of the reader's awakened consciousness, which, sustained by the writing, becomes capable of taking the full measure of things.

Dinah Mulock, the author of *John Halifax, Gentleman* (1857), in the course of a perceptive review shaped by her own religious preoccupations, is troubled specifically by this problem of typicality:

> In the whole history of this fascinating *Maggie* there is a picturesque piteousness which somehow confuses one's sense of right and wrong. Yet what . . . is to become of the hundreds of clever girls, born of uncongenial parents, hemmed in with unsympathising kindred of the Dodson sort, blest with no lover on whom to bestow their strong affections, no friend to whom to cling for guidance and support? They must fight their way, heaven help them! alone and unaided, through cloud and darkness, to the light. And, thank heaven, hundreds of them do, and live to hold out a helping hand afterwards to thousands more.

Maggie's fate, "death, welcomed as the solution to all difficulties, the escape from all pain," troubles Dinah Mulock because it reneges on endurance and companionship—the parallel troubles between the girl in the writing and the girls in the world. She objects to Maggie's escape more than to her conduct. In that, she was rare.

The recoil both from the possibility of Maggie's love for Stephen and from what was seen as the sensuality of George Eliot's writing is a more common response. One reviewer, in particular, feels with a physical shudder the impropriety of conjuring the sensations of the opposite sex:

> But there is a kind of love-making which seems to possess a strange fascination for the modern female novelist. Currer Bell and George Eliot, and we may add George Sand, all like to dwell on love as a strange overmastering force which, through the senses, captivates and enthrals the soul. They linger on the description of the physical sensations that accompany the meeting of hearts of love. Curiously, too, they all like to describe these sensations as they conceive them to exist in men. We are bound to say that their conceptions are true and adequate. But we are not sure that it is quite consistent with feminine delicacy to lay so much stress on the bodily feelings of the other sex. . . . [and] In points like these, it may be observed that men are more delicate than women. There are very few men who would not shrink from putting into words what they might imagine to be the physical effects of love in a woman.

This prurient delicacy, the fear of representing, or of *feeling* what the other sex may feel, sees the woman writer's entry into masculine sensation as a violation of woman's delicacy (and an invasion of the club). The stereotype of separate worlds is used to complain of the sensual description of Maggie's arm, and of Stephen covering it with kisses—a description which doubly affronts, written by a woman, making it plain that arousal crosses sexual difference. Had she represented only Maggie's inner sensations, all might have been well.

We can see in this debate the extent to which George Eliot challenged the boundaries of woman's role by her insistence that the woman novelist should not be confined to imaging women. She denied any exclusive bond between writer and her own sex, even while she acknowledged kinship. Edith Simcox's satisfyingly unexpected characterisation of George Eliot, or Marian Lewes, after her death, emphasises the passion in her nature, "the fulness of life and loving energy that could not accept a lot of negations."

The will to *have,* and not to stand aside, which informs her life beneath its slow surface, is present also in the writing's determination to enter discourse and knowledge attributed to both sexes. And it is there, too, in the narrative energy which sustains diverse possibilities and interactions. In this early book, as in *Scenes of Clerical Life,* the lyrical solution of death is accepted. But later, death never comes at the end of her narrative, at least for her women. They must go on living. The emphasis on laying alongside, on fugitive and sustained analogies between human lots, becomes a means of entering and knowing. Though renunciation is so often her topic, it is not her practice as a novelist.

Chronology

1819   Mary Anne Evans born November 22 on the Arbury estate, Warwickshire, to Robert Evans, carpenter and estate agent, and his wife, Christiana Pearson Evans, daughter of a yeoman farmer.

1824–35   Educated first at a local dame school, then at boarding schools in Attleborough, Nuneaton, and Coventry. In 1832, she witnesses the election riot caused by the first Reform Bill.

1836   Death of mother. Evans and elder sister take over management of the household.

1837   Marriage of elder sister; household management now in Evans's hands. Studies Italian, German, and music under tutors.

1838   Visits London for the first time with her brother Isaac. Schooling has made Evans a zealous Evangelical. Returns to father's house.

1841   Evans and her father move to Coventry. Reads Charles Hennell's *Inquiry into the Origins of Christianity* and Bray's *The Philosophy of Necessity.* Converted from Evangelical Christianity to "a crude state of free-thinking."

1842   Refuses to attend church with her father; later returns to Coventry and to church (although not to her old beliefs).

1843–44   Stays with Dr. and Mrs. Brabant at Devizes. Works on a translation of Strauss's *Das Leben Jesu.* Returns to Coventry, and continues work on the translation (published 1846).

1845   Teaches herself Hebrew.

1849   Death of father. Begins translation of Spinoza's *Tractatus Theologico-Politicus.* Travels to Geneva, where she remains until 1850.

1850–53   Returns to England, becomes assistant (acting) editor of *Westminster Review*. Friendship with Herbert Spencer and George Henry Lewes, critic and author.

1854   Publishes translation of Feuerbach's *The Essence of Christianity*. Takes up residence in Germany with Lewes. Meets Liszt. Begins a translation of Spinoza's *Ethics*.

1855   Returns to England, where she and Lewes take up residence in Richmond. Evans is not received by her family.

1856   Begins to write fiction.

1858   *Scenes of Clerical Life* published under the name George Eliot. Dickens writes Eliot that he is sure she is a woman; her identity is made public after the book is attributed to a dissenting clergyman of Nuneaton.

1859   Publishes *Adam Bede,* which established her as a leading novelist of the day.

1860   Publishes *The Mill on the Floss*.

1861   Publishes *Silas Marner*. Begins writing *Romola*.

1862   Publishes *Romola* serially in *The Cornhill Magazine,* of which Lewes has recently become consulting editor.

1866   Publishes *Felix Holt the Radical*.

1868   Publishes *The Spanish Gypsy*.

1869   Meets John Cross, a wealthy businessman.

1871–72   *Middlemarch* published in parts.

1874   Publishes *The Legend of Jubal and Other Poems*.

1876   Publication of *Daniel Deronda* in parts.

1878   Lewes dies on November 30 of cancer.

1879   Works on preparing edition of essays, *Impressions of Theophrastus Such,* for press. John Blackwood, her publisher, dies on October 29.

1880   Eliot marries John Cross. Dies on December 22 at her home in Cheyne Walk.

1885   John Cross publishes *George Eliot's Life*.

Contributors

HAROLD BLOOM, Sterling Professor of the Humanities at Yale University, is the author of *The Anxiety of Influence, Poetry and Repression,* and many other volumes of literary criticism. His forthcoming study, *Freud: Transference and Authority,* attempts a full-scale reading of all of Freud's major writings. He is the general editor of five series of literary criticism published by Chelsea House. During 1987–88, he served as Charles Eliot Norton Professor of Poetry at Harvard University.

GEORGE LEVINE is Professor of English at Rutgers University. He is the author of *The Boundaries of Fiction: Carlyle, Macaulay, Newman* and, most recently, *The Realistic Imagination.*

U. C. KNOEPFLMACHER is Professor of English at Princeton University. He is the author of *Religious Humanism and the Victorian Novel* and *Laughter and Despair: Readings in Ten Novels of the Victorian Era,* as well as other works.

NINA AUERBACH is Professor of English at the University of Pennsylvania. She is the author of *Woman and the Demon: The Life of a Victorian Myth* and *Romantic Imprisonment: Women and Other Glorified Outcasts.*

MARY JACOBUS is Professor of English and Women's Studies at Cornell University. She is the author of *Tradition and Experiment in Wordsworth's Lyrical Ballads* and the recently published *Reading Woman: Essays in Feminist Criticism.*

DIANNE F. SADOFF is Associate Professor at Colby College. In addition to her book *Monsters of Affection: Dickens, Eliot, and Brontë on Fatherhood,* she has written articles on Victorian poetry.

MARGARET HOMANS is Professor of English at Yale University. She is the author of *Women Writers and Poetic Identity* and *Bearing the Word: Language and Female Experience in Nineteenth-Century Women's Writing.*

GILLIAN BEER is Lecturer in English at Cambridge University. She is best known as the author of *Darwin's Plots: Evolutionary Narrative in Darwin, George Eliot, and Nineteenth-Century Fiction.*

Bibliography

Allott, Miriam. "George Eliot in the 1860's." *Victorian Studies* 5 (1961): 93–108.

Allen, Walter. *George Eliot*. New York: Macmillan, 1964.

Arac, Jonathan. "Rhetoric and Realism in Nineteenth-Century Fiction: Hyperbole in *The Mill on the Floss*." *ELH* 46 (1979): 673–92.

Ashton, Rosemary. *George Eliot*. Past Masters Series. Oxford: Oxford University Press, 1983.

Auerbach, Nina. *Woman and the Demon: The Life of a Victorian Myth*. Cambridge: Harvard University Press, 1982.

Auster, Henry. "George Eliot and the Modern Temper." In *The Worlds of Victorian Fiction*, edited by Jerome H. Buckley, 75–101. Cambridge: Harvard University Press, 1975.

Bedient, Calvin. *Architects of the Self: George Eliot, D. H. Lawrence, and E. M. Forster*. Berkeley and Los Angeles: University of California Press, 1972.

Beer, Gillian. *Darwin's Plots: Evolutionary Narrative in Darwin, George Eliot, and Nineteenth-Century Fiction*. London: Routledge & Kegan Paul, 1983.

Bennett, Joan. *George Eliot: Her Mind and Her Art*. Cambridge: Cambridge University Press, 1948.

Bloom, Harold, ed. *George Eliot: Modern Critical Views*. New Haven: Chelsea House, 1986.

Bonaparte, Felicia. *The Triptych and the Cross: The Central Myths of George Eliot's Poetic Imagination*. New York: New York University Press, 1979.

―――. *Will and Destiny: Morality and Tragedy in George Eliot's Novels*. New York: New York University Press, 1975.

Bullett, Gerald William. *George Eliot: Her Life and Books*. New Haven: Yale University Press, 1948.

Carpenter, Mary Wilson. *George Eliot and the Landscape of Time*. Chapel Hill: University of North Carolina Press, 1986.

Carroll, David, ed. *George Eliot: The Critical Heritage*. London: Routledge & Kegan Paul, 1971.

Christ, Carol. "Aggression and Providential Death in George Eliot's Fiction." *Novel* 9 (1976): 130–40.

Creeger, George R., ed. *George Eliot: A Collection of Critical Essays*. Englewood Cliffs, N.J.: Prentice-Hall, 1970.

Ermarth, Elizabeth Deeds. *George Eliot*. Twayne's English Authors Series. Boston: Twayne, 1985.

Emery, Laura Comer. *George Eliot's Creative Conflict: The Other Side of Silence.* Berkeley and Los Angeles: University of California Press, 1976.

Fisher, Philip. *Making Up Society: The Novels of George Eliot.* Pittsburgh: University of Pittsburgh Press, 1981.

Fulmer, Constance Marie. *George Eliot: A Reference Guide.* Boston: G. K. Hall, 1977.

Gallagher, Catherine. *The Industrial Reformation of English Fiction: Social Discourse and Narrative Form, 1832–1867.* Chicago: University of Chicago Press, 1985.

Gilbert, Sandra M., and Susan Gubar. *The Madwoman in the Attic: The Woman Writer and the Nineteenth-Century Literary Imagination.* New Haven: Yale University Press, 1979.

Graver, Suzanne. *George Eliot and Community: A Study in Social Theory and Fictional Form.* Berkeley and Los Angeles: University of California Press, 1984.

Hagan, John. "A Reinterpretation of *The Mill on the Floss.*" *PMLA* 87 (1972): 53–63.

Haight, Gordon S., ed. *A Century of George Eliot Criticism.* London: Methuen, 1966.

———. *The George Eliot Letters.* New Haven: Yale University Press, 1954.

Haight, Gordon S., and Rosemary T. VanArsdel, eds. *George Eliot: A Centenary Tribute.* Totowa, N.J.: Barnes & Noble, 1982.

Hardy, Barbara. *The Novels of George Eliot: A Study in Form.* London: Athlone, 1959.

———. *Particularities: Readings in George Eliot.* Athens: Ohio University Press, 1983.

———. *Rituals and Feeling in the Novels of George Eliot.* Swansea, U.K.: University College of Swansea, 1973.

———, ed. *Critical Essays on George Eliot.* New York: Barnes & Noble, 1970.

Harvey, William John. *The Art of George Eliot.* New York: Oxford University Press, 1962.

Holmstrom, John, ed. *George Eliot and Her Readers: A Selection of Contemporary Reviews.* New York: Barnes & Noble, 1966.

James, Henry. *Partial Portraits.* London: Macmillan, 1888.

Kenyon, Frank Wilson. *The Consuming Flame: The Story of George Eliot.* New York: Dodd, Mead, 1970.

Knoepflmacher, U. C. *Religious Humanism and the Victorian Novel: George Eliot, Walter Pater, and Samuel Butler.* Princeton: Princeton University Press, 1965.

Kroeber, Karl. *Styles in Fictional Structure: The Art of Jane Austen, Charlotte Brontë, and George Eliot.* Princeton: Princeton University Press, 1971.

Kucich, John. "George Eliot and Objects: Meaning as Matter in *The Mill on the Floss.*" *Dickens Studies Annual* 12 (1983): 319–37.

Leavis, F. R. *The Great Tradition.* London: Chatto & Windus, 1948.

Lee, A. Robert. "*The Mill on the Floss:* Memory and the Reading Experience." In *Reading the Victorian Novel: Detail into Form,* edited by Ian Gregor, 72–91. New York: Barnes & Noble, 1980.

Lerner, Laurence. *The Truthtellers: Jane Austen, George Eliot, D. H. Lawrence.* New York: Schocken, 1967.

Levine, George. *The Realistic Imagination: English Fiction from Frankenstein to Lady Chatterley.* Chicago: University of Chicago Press, 1981.

Liddell, Robert. *The Novels of George Eliot.* New York: St. Martin's, 1977.

Mann, Karen B. *The Language that Makes George Eliot's Fiction.* Baltimore: The Johns Hopkins University Press, 1983.

Martin, Graham. "*The Mill on the Floss* and the Unreliable Narrator." In *George Eliot: Centenary Essays and an Unpublished Fragment,* edited by Anne Smith. New York: Barnes & Noble, 1980.

Miller, J. Hillis. *The Form of Victorian Fiction: Thackeray, Dickens, Trollope, George Eliot, Meredith, and Hardy.* South Bend, Ind.: University of Notre Dame Press, 1968.

———. "The Two Rhetorics: George Eliot's Bestiary." In *Writing and Reading Differently: Deconstruction and the Teaching of Composition and Literature,* edited by G. Douglas Atkins and Michael L. Johnson, 101–14. Lawrence: University Press of Kansas, 1985.

Miller, Nancy K. "Emphasis Added: Plots and Plausibilities in Women's Fiction." *PMLA* 96 (1981): 36–48.

Mintz, Alan L. *George Eliot and the Novel of Vocation.* Cambridge: Harvard University Press, 1978.

New, Peter. *Fiction and Purpose in* Utopia, Rasselas, The Mill on the Floss, *and* Women in Love. New York: St. Martin's, 1985.

Paris, Bernard J. *Experiments in Life: George Eliot's Quest for Values.* Detroit: Wayne State University Press, 1965.

———. "The Inner Conflicts of Maggie Tulliver: A Horneyan Analysis." *The Centennial Review* 13 (1969): 166–99.

Peterson, Carla. "The Heroine as Reader in the Nineteenth-Century Novel: Emma Bovary and Maggie Tulliver." *Comparative Literature Studies* 17 (1980): 168–83.

Pinney, Thomas, ed. *The Essays of George Eliot.* New York: Columbia University Press, 1963.

Putzell, Sara M. "'An Antagonism of Valid Claims': The Dynamics of *The Mill on the Floss.*" *Studies in the Novel* 7 (1975): 227–44.

Redinger, Ruby V. *George Eliot: The Emergent Self.* New York: Knopf, 1975.

Roberts, Lynne Tidaback. "Perfect Pyramids: *The Mill on the Floss.*" *Texas Studies in Literature and Language* 13 (1971): 111–24.

Sadoff, Dianne F. *Monsters of Affection: Dickens, Eliot, and Brontë on Fatherhood.* Baltimore: The Johns Hopkins University Press, 1982.

Schleifer, Ronald. "Irony and the Literary Past: On *The Concept of Irony* and *The Mill on the Floss.*" In *Kierkegaard and Literature: Irony, Repetition, and Criticism,* edited by Ronald Schleifer and Robert Markley, 183–216. Norman: University of Oklahoma Press, 1984.

Showalter, Elaine. "The Greening of Sister George." *Nineteenth-Century Fiction* 35 (1980): 292–311.

———. *A Literature of Their Own: British Women Novelists from Brontë to Lessing.* Princeton: Princeton University Press, 1977.

Smalley, Barbara. *George Eliot and Flaubert: Pioneers of the Modern Novel.* Athens: Ohio University Press, 1974.

Speight, Robert. *George Eliot.* London: Barker, 1968.

Stephen, Leslie. *George Eliot.* New York: AMS, 1973.

Stone, Donald D. *The Romantic Impulse in Victorian Fiction.* Cambridge: Harvard University Press, 1980.

Stump, Reva. *Movement and Vision in George Eliot's Novels.* Seattle: University of Washington Press, 1959.

Wasserman, Renata R. Mautner. "Narrative Logic and the Form of Tradition in *The Mill on the Floss*." *Studies in the Novel* 14 (1982): 266–79.

Welsh, Alexander. *George Eliot and Blackmail*. Cambridge: Harvard University Press, 1985.

Woolf, Virginia. "George Eliot." In *The Common Reader: First Series*. New York: Harcourt, Brace & World, 1925.

Acknowledgments

"Intelligence as Deception: *The Mill on the Floss*" by George Levine from *PMLA* 80, no. 4 (September 1965), © 1965 by the Modern Language Association of America. Reprinted by permission of the Modern Language Association of America.

"Tragedy and the Flux: *The Mill on the Floss*" by U. C. Knoepflmacher from *George Eliot's Early Novels: The Limits of Realism* by U. C. Knoepflmacher, © 1968 by the Regents of the University of California. Reprinted by permission of the University of California Press.

"The Power of Hunger: Demonism and Maggie Tulliver" by Nina Auerbach from *Nineteenth-Century Fiction* 30, no. 2 (September 1975), © 1975 by the Regents of the University of California. Reprinted by permission of the University of California Press.

"The Question of Language: Men of Maxims and *The Mill on the Floss*" by Mary Jacobus from *Critical Inquiry* 8, no. 2 (Winter 1981), © 1981 by the University of Chicago. Reprinted by permission of the author and the University of Chicago Press.

"George Eliot: The Law and the Father" (originally entitled "The Law and the Father") by Dianne F. Sadoff from *Monsters of Affection: Dickens, Eliot, and Brontë on Fatherhood* by Diane F. Sadoff, © 1982 by the Johns Hopkins University Press, Baltimore / London. Reprinted by permission of the Johns Hopkins University Press.

"Eliot, Wordsworth, and the Scenes of the Sisters' Instruction" by Margaret Homans from *Bearing the Word: Language and Female Experience in Nineteenth-Century Women's Writing* by Margaret Homans, © 1986 by the University of Chicago. Reprinted by permission of the author and the University of Chicago Press.

" 'The Dark Woman Triumphs': Passion in *The Mill on the Floss*" by Gillian Beer from *George Eliot* (Key Women Writers Series), edited by Sue Rose, © 1986 by Gillian Beer. Reprinted by permission of the Harvester Press Ltd. and Indiana University Press.

151

Index

DATE DUE